M000093600

A WEEKLY Letter to Your MISSIONARY

MESSAGES
TO INSPIRE AND STRENGTHEN
ELDERS AND SISTERS

JEFFREY ERICKSON

CFI, AN IMPRINT OF CEDAR FORT, INC.
SPRINGVILLE, UTAH

To Christine—my wife, best friend,
eternal companion, and the mother and "trainer" of
some of the greatest missionaries I have ever known.

© 2017 Jeffrey Erickson
All rights reserved.

No part of this book may be reproduced in any form whatsoever, whether by graphic, visual, electronic, film, microfilm, tape recording, or any other means, without prior written permission of the publisher, except in the case of brief passages embodied in critical reviews and articles.

This is not an official publication of The Church of Jesus Christ of Latter-day Saints. The opinions and views expressed herein belong solely to the author and do not necessarily represent the opinions or views of Cedar Fort, Inc. Permission for the use of sources, graphics, and photos is also solely the responsibility of the author.

ISBN 13: 978-1-4621-2028-4

Published by CFI, an imprint of Cedar Fort, Inc.
2373 W. 700 S., Springville, UT 84663
Distributed by Cedar Fort, Inc., www.cedarfort.com

LIBRARY OF CONGRESS CATALOGING-IN-PUBLICATION DATA ON FILE

Cover design by Kinsey Beckett
Cover design © 2017 by Cedar Fort, Inc.
Typeset by Chelsea Holdaway

Printed in the United States of America

10 9 8 7 6 5 4 3 2 1

Printed on acid-free paper

CONTENTS

COMING TO THE SAVIOR

BECOMING A BETTER TEACHER

SERVING LIKE THE SAVIOR

FOR TIMES OF TRIAL

DILIGENCE IS KEY

REMEMBER, YOU ARE NOT ALONE

IT'S ALL ABOUT LOVE

FINDING STRENGTH BEYOND YOUR OWN

POWERFUL PRAYER

PROMISED BLESSINGS

ACKNOWLEDGMENTS

I am forever grateful to the missionary program of The Church of Jesus Christ of Latter-day Saints. Despite being removed from a full-time mission for many years, the memories are etched in my mind forever. I am grateful to every companion, leader, and missionary I served with in the Canada Halifax Mission so many years ago.

The only misprint in this book is on the cover because I am the only recognized author; my wife, Christine, should also be recognized on the cover because she sacrificed more than I did by allowing me to take the time to write this book. I am grateful to her as my coauthor, inspiration, and helpmeet. The greatest blessing of my life has been to serve with her as my companion in a variety of callings and other meaningful opportunities.

I am extremely grateful to Holly Banks for her belief in these weekly letters. I am thankful for her skills and insights in editing and proofing and in pushing me to publish this work. She has been a trusted friend with valued opinions and support. I am also grateful to Marjorie Eddy Harris for her work in the first editing process. She helped keep this book alive in its beginning stages.

I am grateful to Cedar Fort, and to all the wonderful staff who have given the book a chance to succeed and bless the lives of missionaries around the world.

I am grateful for the opportunity to read the Book of Mormon constantly during the writing process. Nearly all of these letters stem from the principles, phrases, and doctrines of that sacred record.

This book is dedicated to the modern missionaries of our day who still go out two by two, proclaiming the good news of the gospel of Jesus Christ.

INTRODUCTION

A few years ago in Arizona, on a hot Sunday afternoon in August, my wife left church early with our new baby. The only possible ride home for my other children was with me after church, but I had to participate in a setting apart. I told my four boys it would be at least fifteen minutes before I was ready to go home. I gave them the keys to the car and told them to get in and turn on the car's air conditioning so they wouldn't be hot while they waited for me. I participated in the setting apart and headed out to the car about fifteen to twenty minutes later.

As I walked to the car, I thought they must have gotten a ride because I couldn't hear the car engine running. Approaching the car, I found the boys inside, but the car was not on, and only the little fan motor was running. They had put the keys in the ignition and turned on the air, but had never started the motor. I looked into the car to see four boys (ages eleven, eight, six, and four) sweating profusely. My four-year-old McKay was in the backseat taking off his shirt because he was so hot. For fifteen minutes, they all had been sitting in 108-degree heat with a small car fan circulating the hot air.

After observing them for a moment and realizing they were not in danger, I laughed at their plight and explained that to get cold air the engine must be running. For me, it was a rather humorous lesson in teaching and instruction. I quickly learned that one piece of instruction can make a great deal of difference in our lives. It is for this reason that I have written this missionary book. I hope that one small detail—one verse, one quote, one story, or one principle of truth—in the pages of this book will make a difference in the life of a missionary.

Throughout my adult life, Monday has typically been my least favorite day of the week; as it has always meant going back to "the grind" and starting another workweek. I am amazed at how having a missionary serving full-time has transformed my Mondays. It has quickly become a favorite day of the week for my wife and me. Every Monday there is the anticipation surrounding the long-awaited missionary email. On numerous occasions, we have checked our inbox at least a dozen times before receiving "good news from afar." What a blessing it is to receive even a short paragraph from a young son or daughter who is serving the Lord with all his or her heart, might, mind, and strength. What a blessing to witness the changes that take place over the course of a mission in a young man or young woman's life.

A few years ago when I was called to be bishop of our ward, I began writing monthly letters to our full-time missionaries. After a while, the letters became mini-sermons and more meaningful to me because I could see how they strengthened those individuals in the mission field. Finally, when my own son left for his mission, I began to write a weekly letter. This weekly letter became a labor of love for me as I studied the Book of Mormon daily; allowing passages and phrases to fill my mind with topics and principles to cover. I was amazed at how missionary-centered the Book of Mormon became for me. I was also grateful for the lessons the Spirit taught me personally as I wrote about Book of Mormon doctrines, phrases, principles, and topics. The entire experience reminded me of the "great worth" of the principles in the Book of Mormon.

In this book, I have attempted to address topics that missionaries deal with daily. I have tried to allow you, the reader, to receive a prompting for your missionary regarding a specific topic or letter you feel would be a blessing to them at a certain time. I believe that in this way you can play an active role in their mission as the need arises. Heavenly Father is teaching them lesson after lesson, day after day, but you can find joy in receiving impressions and promptings for your missionary as you prayerfully write to them each week.

I have wondered why I felt inspired to write this book, as it has taken so much time, energy, and effort. My wife and family have sacrificed to give me the time I needed to write this book, and I am grateful for their love and support. I believe there are two reasons why I felt the need to write *A Weekly Letter to Your Missionary*. The first is that "sometimes it is hard being a missionary."[1] The second reason comes from Moroni. I have felt in a small way, a little of what Moroni felt when he said, "Wherefore, I, Moroni, am commanded to write these things that evil may be done away, and that the time may come that Satan may have no power upon the hearts of the children of men, but that they may be persuaded to do good continually, that they may come unto the fountain of all righteousness and be saved" (Ether 8:26). My hope is that these words which I have written will aid in the removal of evil, so that Satan will have no power over the hearts of the elders and sisters, and that missionaries will be persuaded to do good. I hope that with the help of this book, missionaries throughout the world will come unto the fountain of all righteousness, which is Christ, and that they will more effectively invite others to do the same.

To every missionary, or family member of a missionary, who reads this book, I echo the words of Mormon: "My son [or daughter], be faithful in Christ; and may not the things which I have written grieve thee, to weigh thee down unto death; but may Christ lift thee up, and may his sufferings and death, and the showing his body unto our fathers, and his mercy and long-suffering, and the hope of his glory and of eternal life, rest in your mind forever" (Moroni 9:25).

Your friend,
Brother Jeff Erickson

NOTES

1. Jeffrey R. Holland, "The Cost—and Blessings—of Discipleship," *Ensign*, May 2014.

START STRONG

Dear Elders and Sisters,

One of the fastest races in the world is usually run indoors. The event is the sixty-meter dash, and, among the world's elite, it is usually over in less than seven seconds. This event hasn't been run in the Olympics since 1904, but if you ever get a chance to watch the world's fastest in this event, you will be inspired and impressed. Along with having world-class speed, a precise and fast start is paramount in this event. Slow starts in this sixty-meter race often eliminate even the fastest of runners. In a sixty-meter race, I don't believe that the fastest runner always wins; rather, the one with the *most exceptional start* usually creates the best opportunity for victory.

As a missionary in the MTC, I hope you have a fast start. I hope you are able to hit the ground running: studying, praying, learning, pondering, teaching, and testifying, and doing all of this while being diligent and faithful. You will establish great patterns in the MTC. The next phase of your mission (after the MTC) will be critical: the transition back to the real world with your first real companion. Do everything you can to keep your exceptional habits from the MTC and continue to build upon those meaningful daily practices. In your first area, things will be different. There may not be other missionaries, outside of your companion, to lean on. Your first companion in the field may be wonderful, they may be lazy, they may be hardworking, or they may just do whatever you do. An important attribute that every missionary must develop in order to start fast is courage. Elder Marvin J. Ashton pleaded, "God give us the courage to act now."[1] Missionaries who act in the now will have fast starts.

The first three days of my mission after the MTC were some of the most trying days of my entire mission. My first companion was a great elder, but the missionary who trained him hadn't been extremely motivated. My companion had surrendered some of his original missionary standards, dreams, and ideals. He had wanted to be a great missionary when he entered his first area, but by following his trainer, he had let go of some important personal goals, desires, and habits. I arrived, and he continued to do what he had been trained to do, which was very little. After three days of wasting time, my frustration was close to boiling over when, finally, we had a big companionship inventory, and we established wonderful goals and objectives.

Our new goals required difficult changes and stretching from both of us. It wasn't easy, and we weren't without struggles, but we started working more diligently and successfully. We were soon working hard, teaching numerous lessons, and finding many interested investigators. The work began to blossom in an area where the work had once been slow. We had a wonderful month together after those first few excruciating days. I will be forever grateful to my companion for his willingness to allow our companionship to make adjustments, change our direction, and work hard, as we had been off to a slow start.

I share that experience, not to blame our slothfulness on my companion, but to inform you that you need to be ready for anything in the first area of your mission. On day one, you may be confronted with some shocking bad habits or practices. You need to be willing to boldly and kindly stand and say, "we need to do more and be better." I hope you get an awesome companion, and that they will show you how to be an effective instrument in the hands of a loving God. I hope that you will start teaching, finding, activating, and baptizing from hour one in your first area. I pray that if you get there and all is not well in Zion, that you will help to make Zion (your area and your companionship) prosper again.

I have observed that, like running a sixty-meter dash, one of the keys to a successful mission experience is a fast start. I challenge you to make your first month one of the best months of your mission. President Henry B. Eyring said, "Learning to start early and to be steady are the keys to spiritual preparation."[2] You will arrive from the MTC full of the spirit of God, the spirit of enthusiasm, and the faith to see miracles happen right away. Let that powerful spirit motivate you to do great things from the very beginning of your service. No missionary needs a trial month. Missionaries need to hit the pavement running and feel the blessings of faithful service right away. Your first area will seem like a dream later in your mission, so start fast and make the most of it.

Here is one recurring observation from my mission: a missionary's first month in the field frequently dictated how they served the rest of their mission. I observed missionary patterns established in those first few months, for better or worse, that seemed to continue throughout entire missions. I observed great elders and sisters come from the MTC and get shattered by a difficult first companion and never seem to recover throughout their mission. I saw great missionaries with wonderful trainers serve incredible missions. I saw other missionaries, no matter who their companion was, just work hard and have success throughout their entire missions. I saw others who were wonderful missionaries become complacent and go home with much regret.

In the National Hockey League (NHL), the first team to score wins 67 percent of the time.[3] In other sports, like soccer and football, the odds of winning increase when a team "starts fast" and scores first. When a missionary is committed to starting his or her mission effectively, there is an increased likelihood of establishing powerful habits and dominant patterns.

As a missionary, you will find that it is critical to start strong in your first area. You will use that strong start as a foundation for the rest of your mission. Elder Marvin J. Ashton said, "How unwise we are to waste our todays when they determine the significance of our tomorrows."[4] I pray your today will be powerful, so that your tomorrow can be peaceful.

I believe transition points in life are critical adjustment periods. The transition you made from being a teenager, a full-time employee, a high school senior, or a college student to being a missionary in the MTC should have been handled beautifully, and you should have made critical adjustments. If not, start now to become the kind of missionary you want to be and finish strong. Remember that Alma, after numerous negative experiences in Ammonihah, was cast out of the city. He was then visited by an angel and told to go back. His immediate response

Key Missionary Moments

is inspirational as he "returned speedily" to Ammonihah (Alma 8:18). Despite a slow start in Ammonihah, he went back and through persistent effort was blessed with success.

As a bishop I noticed a very simple pattern in my ward, with a limited number of exceptions. The members of my ward who came to church the earliest, were in their seats before the meeting started, and who had the "best seats," were the ones who were the most active, the most involved, and seemed to have the best experiences in church. These members who literally started earlier and faster seemed to be blessed with a much greater Sunday religious experience and seemed to be in better spiritual health. I believe a mission is the same way for those who start earlier, faster, and stronger; they are in better spiritual health.

I am certain that within thirty days of being in your first area, you will have already witnessed the miracle of the Atonement in someone's life. May you continue to be in good spiritual health and witness the miracle of the Atonement in your life, and may you start early, fast, and strong in His service.

Your friend,
Brother Jeff Erickson

NOTES

1. Marvin J. Ashton, "The Time Is Now," *Ensign*, May 1975.
2. Henry B. Eyring, "Spiritual Preparedness: Start Early and Be Steady," *Ensign*, November 2005.
3. "The value of the first goal," Eric T., *SB Nation*, October 22, 2013, www .sbnation.com/nhl/2013/10/22/4830198.
4. Ashton, "The Time Is Now."

KNOW WHO YOU ARE

Dear Elders and Sisters,

After my mission, when I was a student at BYU, I taught at the MTC. Teaching there was a very rich and rewarding experience, and it kept me in tune with the spirit of my mission. One of the MTC mission presidents while I taught there was Brother Ed Pinegar. He was a great man: full of life and full of the Spirit. One of the things he spoke about frequently was knowing who you are. When he would meet many of the missionaries, he would often say, "Don't you know who I am? I am Heavenly Father's boy!" What a great title, and what a great understanding of who he was. I have thought about those words and that title—"Heavenly Father's boy"—many times. I have concluded that there is immense power in really knowing who we are and who our Heavenly Father is.

When Moses went up into an exceedingly high mountain, he saw God face to face. (See Moses 1:1–2.) He had a life-changing experience as he found out who he was and saw the workmanship of God's hands. He learned that Christ would be the Savior, and he learned that he was a son of God. Three times the Lord called Moses "my son" (Moses 1:6, 7, 40). The Lord showed Moses the creation of the world and all of the children of men. Following this remarkable experience, "Moses was left unto himself" (Moses 1:9). Satan came to him after Moses's remarkable experience, "And it came to pass that when Moses had said these words, behold, Satan came tempting him, saying: Moses, son of man, worship me" (Moses 1:12). There is majesty in Moses's response: "And it came to pass that Moses looked upon Satan and said: Who art thou? For behold, I am a Son of God, in the similitude of his Only Begotten; and where is thy glory, that I should worship thee?" (Moses 1:13). It was almost as if Moses was saying, "Don't you know who I am? I am a son of God created in His image; why would you ever

9

try to tempt me?" I love this powerful response. His reply is a reminder to me of the power of being a son or daughter of God.

Moses continued to draw power and strength from his recent experience and knowledge as he said, "Get thee hence, Satan; deceive me not; for God said unto me: Thou art after the similitude of mine Only Begotten" (Moses 1:16). Again, Moses shows his understanding that he is like or similar to the Son of God. Moses is able to draw great strength from knowing who he really is. We, like Moses, are in the similitude of Christ; do we draw power from that knowledge?

We often sing the Primary song, "I am a Child of God." There are some wonderful insights that are shared in the words of that song. The best part is found in the powerful title. When I sing those treasured words, I can feel what God wants me to know about who I am.

The prophet Nephi said, "I know he [the Lord] loveth his children; nevertheless, I do not know the meaning of all things" (1 Nephi 11:17). When we know God loves us, we can draw power and peace from that knowledge. When we know who we really are, we can see that life has a purpose. When we know who we are, we can have strength like Moses to say, "Get thee hence, Satan." When we know who we are, we are filled with hope, light, optimism, and direction. When we know who we are, we press forward with steadfastness in Christ. When missionaries know who they are, they testify of God and Christ with authenticity.

Years ago, I read about a culture in South America where when someone is found guilty of a crime, he is not punished. Instead, the guilty party is brought in front of all the people, and the people stand around and begin telling good stories about him. They try to get the offender to remember who he really is. They talk about all the good things the person has done in the past. They remind the person of who he has been and what he can be again.

I believe our Heavenly Father is the same way. He wants us to remember where we came from. He wants us to remember our potential. He wants us to remember our great worth. He wants us to remember that we are His children. May you remember that you are a child of God, and that He is your Father.

Your friend,
Brother Jeff Erickson

PIVOTAL MOMENTS

Dear Elders and Sisters,

This week I want to talk about pivotal moments. Let me share an example of what I mean by a pivotal moment. On the night of April 14, 1912, the ocean liner *Californian* was 1,500 miles from Boston Harbor. A ship nine miles away was sending up rocket flares that seemed to be distress signals. The crew on the *Californian* attempted to send a message through their Morse lamp, but there was no response from the other ship. The captain of the *Californian* watched through binoculars, and the distant ship appeared to sail away as its lights vanished in the distance one by one. Meanwhile, the ship nine miles away was sending distress signals not by Morse lamp, but by radio. The *Californian* was within range of those urgent radio signals, but their radio operator had turned off the radio and was fast asleep in his cabin. The ship nine miles away was the *Titanic*.[1]

There are important events and decisions made at critical junctures in our lives, and these are pivotal moments in our mortal existence. Elder Holland, quoting a young father said, "Perhaps our most pivotal moments as Latter-day Saints come when we have to swim directly against the current of the culture in which we live."[2]

At my mother's seventy-fifth birthday party, I saw the parents of two of my high school friends. I inquired about the well-being of both friends, and I was struck by the polarity of their situations. I want to share with you what has transpired in the lives of these two friends over the last thirty years.

The first friend is Michael (name changed). He was a good kid in high school. He was very intelligent, fun loving, and kind. He wasn't a star athlete in high school, but he was a talented, nice kid. When the appropriate time came, he went on a mission and served faithfully. After his full-time service, he went to BYU, excelled there, and then went to law school. Now, he is an extremely successful attorney with a large corporation. He married a faithful and fantastic woman, and they have wonderful children. He has remained very active in the Church and is devoted to the Lord, his family, and his work.

When I asked Michael's mother how he was doing, she glowingly said, "wonderful." Although the response was simple, it was powerful. I knew Michael was doing "wonderful" because I had witnessed Michael make excellent critical decisions during many pivotal moments in his life. In high school, when some of his buddies were having inappropriate relationships with girls, he chose not to. The opportunities were there, but he always chose to abstain. When there was peer pressure to make a poor choice, Michael seemed to rise above those temptations and choose wisely. Michael could have gone to any college in the country, including the Ivy League schools, because of his exceptional grades and top scores on the entrance exams. Michael chose BYU for the university's environment and the comfort he felt there. His mission was another critical decision at a pivotal time for Michael, and he served a terrific mission to Mexico.

Michael has always been a fun person filled with confidence and intelligence, and he has gratefully taken what the Lord has allotted him, using his gifts and talents wisely. He has been exceedingly blessed by a loving Heavenly Father. I am certain Michael has had his fair share of life challenges, but I will say that when pivotal and critical moments have come in his life, he has made great decisions. I am sure it wasn't always easy, and I am certain he has not been perfect, but the Lord has blessed him and his good family for his critical decisions in pivotal moments. Michael has been a great example and an inspiration to me for years, even though he probably never knew that.

The second parent I ran into at the party was Chuck's mom (name changed). I asked her how Chuck was. She said, "Oh, you know Chuck. He just got divorced for the second time. All of his kids are out of the Church, and they are a mess. He is out of the Church too." Chuck is the oldest brother in a big family. All but two of the siblings are currently less-active in the Church. Chuck was the leader of his family, and his siblings looked up to him as their role model.

If there was anyone I would have chosen to be back in high school, it would have been Chuck. He was incredibly athletic, fast, strong, popular, handsome, confident, and fun. Chuck was probably the envy of every young man. He had so much going for him. Chuck could have been anyone or done anything with his charisma, talents, and abilities. Chuck made a few great decisions in his life, but he also made some bad ones at pivotal moments.

During many crucial periods of his life, Chuck fell into the adversary's traps of temptation and sin. In high school, all the girls loved Chuck, and he fell into the trap of immorality. Chuck made the wonderful decision to repent and go on a mission. He served an incredible mission. His letters were full of the Spirit and were inspiring. Yet, when he returned home, prior patterns returned. He made uninspired decisions at critical times and they greatly impacted his future.

When Chuck came home, he put himself in inappropriate environments. He went back to his prior inappropriate habits and sins, which distracted Chuck from things of faith and things of great worth. He met a good young lady whom he married outside of the temple. They struggled together and were eventually divorced. He was a devoted father, but he became less active in the Church at a pivotal time for his children. He married again outside of the Church, and, again, things didn't work out and they were divorced. Chuck had some pivotal periods in his life, which required good and powerful critical decisions, and he chose poorly. Those decisions in pivotal moments have brought him unrest, unhappiness, despair, and sorrow. When Chuck needed to step up and make great decisions, he usually didn't. He cowered to the world, the adversary, and short-term decisions that brought temporary pleasure, but not lasting happiness.

Returning from the party, the contrast of these two conversations pricked my spirit. I awoke the next morning after talking to these two mothers and was greatly troubled. Both of these individuals came from quality families. Chuck was faster, stronger, more athletic, and more handsome than Michael or me. He had so many gifts and talents. All of his potential was lost because Chuck forgot who he was and what his life's purpose was. At critical junctures in his life, he turned left instead of right. He followed the lusts of the flesh instead of the Spirit of God.

There will be times in your life, where the Spirit says, "Now is the time." The Spirit will say, "Don't do this," or "Stay away from that." When the Spirit directs you in pivotal moments, you must go and do. Chuck rejected the Spirit at pivotal times and has paid a heavy price. Michael, on the other hand, acted when the Spirit directed him and has been blessed by the Lord accordingly.

By sharing these experiences, I am not saying that we will never have trials or troubles or commit sins if we are faithful—that is not the truth. I know these things happen to both the faithful and the unfaithful. I am only saying that when we make good decisions at pivotal times, we are entitled to the Lord's richest blessings.

As a missionary, there will be pivotal moments during your mission where you will feel the promptings of the Holy Ghost directing you to take action. These significant instances will make the difference between being a servant of God who follows the Spirit, and being a regular missionary who succumbs to the will of the flesh. A servant of God is one who turns their life over to God and serves selflessly. Be a servant of God. Turn your will, your life, your time, your talents, and your heart over to God.

Your friend,
Brother Jeff Erickson

NOTES

1. Paul Harvey Jr., *More of Paul Harvey's The Rest of the Story* (Bantam, 1984), 1–2.
2. Jeffrey R. Holland, "'Like a Watered Garden,'" *Ensign*, November 2001.

THE PERFECT DAY

Dear Elders and Sisters,

There is a phrase found in Doctrine and Covenants 50:24 which I hope is indicative of every day of your mission: "That which is of God is light; and he that receiveth light, and continueth in God, receiveth more light; and that light groweth brighter and brighter until *the perfect day*" (emphasis added). I hope that on each day of your mission, the light in you grows and grows until "the perfect day." I hope that most days of your mission feel like "the perfect day."

What is "the perfect day" as a missionary? Is it teaching five Spirit-filled lessons? Is it finding a wonderful, golden family to teach? Is it feeling the Spirit testify of your message? Is it when the Spirit puts words in your mouth that you know are not your own? Is it testifying of a principle and having the Spirit reaffirm to you that the principle is true? Is it telling the story of Joseph Smith and feeling the fire burn inside your soul and knowing that he truly was a prophet of God? Is it when you speak of the Atonement of Jesus Christ and you can barely speak because you are so grateful for this precious gift?

I recall many days during the course of my mission that felt like perfect days. Here is one perfect day that I love to reflect upon. My companion and I were teaching the wonderful White family, when the Spirit said, "invite them to be baptized." I invited the father Robert to be baptized, and he said, "Yes." I then invited his good wife, Carolyn, and she said, "I am not ready." Then we invited their oldest son, Jason. He said, "Yes." His mom was shocked that her fourteen-year-old son had a desire to be baptized. She quickly asked Jason, "Why do you want to be baptized?" Jason powerfully bore his testimony and said, "Mom, you know how it feels when you win the championship baseball game? That is how I feel—only better—when the missionaries come and teach our family." The mother, after hearing Jason's words, quickly recanted and said she, too, wanted to be baptized. Two other brothers, Dawson and Tyson, also committed to baptism, while young Robin would have to wait until he turned eight. I will always remember that day of my mission as one of those perfect days where light is given and light is received. That light grew brighter and brighter for myself, my companion, and the White family that day.

I am so thankful for perfect days. I believe in my life as a missionary, father, teacher, bishop, and son of God, that I have had many perfect days. They have inspired, blessed, changed, and motivated me to be more obedient and faithful. I feel there is nothing better than a perfect day, and I will always long for more.

I remember a perfect day I had as a father. It was a few days before my son Tyler left for college. I had the opportunity to give him a priesthood blessing. I believe it is so difficult to send a child away because, as a parent, you feel you can't do much for them. I didn't feel the emptiness of those feelings however. With a special family meeting and a priesthood blessing, I felt that we could do a lot for him. A few days later, Tyler said that during the blessing, he didn't feel the Spirit. After the blessing, he went down to his room, and things changed. The Spirit began to penetrate his heart, and he began to cry. With the Spirit present in his room, he made some important commitments to himself and to God.

I remember a perfect day I had as a bishop. A married couple had come to my office, and told me they were done. The wife was ready for a divorce, but was willing to make one last-ditch effort to meet with the bishop. Her husband had been selfish and was not doing his part in the marriage, and she couldn't handle it anymore. I started to talk to this couple, and I started to draw on the whiteboard in my office. I was not even certain what I would say. As I continued to draw and talk, words and ideas from the Spirit came to me, and I shared them with these two people in this extremely damaged relationship. I had drawn a diagram that continued to come together as we discussed the relationship. The Spirit was present, and they were both touched. The husband said, "Bishop, this makes sense. I can do this." He left the office with a new determination. The wife also left with a renewed hope. I left my office that day knowing that the Lord had taught all of us through the Spirit. We all received light that day, and we all understood and were all edified. The beauty of this story is that that couple is still married and is doing much better; they have put their trust in a loving God who cares about their marriage.

I remember a perfect day I had as a teacher. I had been asked to speak to a few hundred youth and was a bit overwhelmed with the assignment. I had been praying about how to approach the youth on a difficult topic, but I had no ideas or answers. I studied and prepared for some time and still had no real ideas or answers coming to me. I pressed forward and was rewarded with a wonderful insight as I came across a story that put the entire subject into perspective with a tremendous analogy. The story made the topic come to life, and I was able to draw powerful parallels that were able to carry my message to the hearts of my listeners more effectively. I was so grateful for the guidance and impressions that helped me understand the topic better and teach the subject more powerfully. I was so edified by the light that came to me during that preparation time.

May you have many perfect days, full of light, and may they get brighter and brighter until every day is a perfect day.

Your friend,
Brother Jeff Erickson

FINISH STRONG

Dear Elders and Sisters,

The Masters Golf Tournament is one of the biggest tournaments in professional golf. In the 2016 Masters Golf Tournament, Jordan Spieth—one of the best golfers in the world—had the lead at the end of the first day. He also held the lead after the second and third day. On the fourth and final day, Spieth's lead was swelling as he played steady and terrific golf. With nine holes left, Spieth had increased his lead to five strokes. He simply needed to steadily play his game; he was literally in the driver's seat with almost no possible way to lose.

Spieth bogeyed the next two holes. At the par-three twelfth hole, he was still leading the field by three strokes. On the short par-three, he put his golf ball in the water in front of the green twice, and he took a quadruple bogey seven. He walked off the twelve green, now out of the lead, and he never recovered. He lost the Masters championship by three strokes.[1] Could that happen to any golfer? Yes. Does it happen often? No! Did Jordan have the ability and talent to finish strong? Yes! What happened to one of the best golfers in the world on those back nine holes? I don't know, but I would like to make one observation.

Here is the parallel. In this tournament, Jordan Spieth did not finish the way he started. He started strong, played well, but desperately struggled during the last nine holes. Are we all guilty of this in our lives? Probably. As a missionary, the question I pose today is *will you finish strong?* Will you be antsy and not completely effective in the last few months of your mission? Or will you get stronger toward your last few weeks, utilizing the lessons, principles, and wisdom you have accumulated during your mission, or will you waver in your commitment? I pray that you will only enhance your efforts in your remaining time.

During my full-time mission, I observed missionaries of both parties. I saw many missionaries who diligently worked through the last hours of their full-time service. Unfortunately, I also observed other missionaries who seemed to be done with their service, despite being assigned for a few more months. Remember, you were called to serve for a full eighteen or twenty-four months. There is no excuse to forget how important your service is, or to relax or slow in your efforts as your mission comes to a close.

The scriptures are full of examples of faithful people who finished strong. The first person that comes to my mind is Abinadi because he literally testified until his final dying breath. He didn't sit in prison and relax because his earthly mission time was coming to a close, he diligently continued teaching. Mormon, who was writing to let his son know that he was still alive, gave this powerful directive: "And now, my beloved son, notwithstanding their hardness, let us labor diligently; for if we should cease to labor, we should be brought under condemnation; for we have a labor to perform whilst in this tabernacle of clay, that we may conquer the enemy of all righteousness, and rest our souls in the kingdom of God" (Moroni 9:6). Here, Mormon was fighting for his life, near the end of his life, but his purpose was to remind his son to labor diligently. His words are a call to finish strong.

I am certain that Moroni in Mormon chapter eight felt alone when he wrote of his dire situation: "And my father also was killed by them, and I even remain alone to write the sad tale of the destruction of my people. But behold, they are gone, and I fulfill the commandment of my father. And whether they will slay me, I know not" (Mormon 8:3). He continues on and says: "And behold, I would write it also if I had room upon the plates, but I have not; and ore I have none, for I am alone. My father hath been slain in battle, and all my kinsfolk, and I have not friends nor whither to go; and how long the Lord will suffer that I may live I know not" (Mormon 8:5). You can almost sense a discouragement or a bit of a breaking will in his words, but that is not who Moroni is. He shares his very personal feelings about his difficult state and then he moves on. It is just a few verses later when he testifies powerfully: "For the eternal purposes of the Lord shall roll on, until all his promises shall be fulfilled" (Mormon 8:22). This is the Moroni

I love; he is saying no matter how bleak the outlook, God will fulfill every promise.

After this great chapter, Moroni carried on in the work of the Lord. He recorded many more precious things. He gave us the ninth chapter of Mormon, which is a powerful treatise on miracles. He then abridged the book of Ether. Then he wrote, or recorded, the final ten chapters of Moroni. He did most of this despite feeling like he might not live to record any more on the precious plates. He said, "Wherefore, I write a few more things, contrary to that which I had supposed; for I had supposed not to have written any more; but I write a few more things, that perhaps they may be of worth unto my brethren, the Lamanites, in some future day, according to the will of the Lord" (Moroni 1:4). I am so grateful that Moroni didn't casually finish his ministry. I am grateful that he didn't say, "I already told people I was done, so I am not writing any more." I am grateful that many of the best chapters in the Book of Mormon were given to us after the miraculous preservation of his life.

Without Moroni finishing strong, the sacred Book of Mormon promise would not have been written. If Moroni had not finished strong, we would not have the greatest treatise ever written on charity. Without Moroni finishing his work, we would not have insights on the light of Christ. Without Moroni's finishing touches we would not have been encouraged to "lay hold on every good thing" (Moroni 7:21). There are so many final pieces of wisdom that Moroni shared, that would have been lost if he had not finished strong. I am so grateful that Moroni endured to the end in his writing as I, and millions of others, have been blessed by his efforts.

Just as Moroni finished strong, you can and should do the same on your mission. Finishing strong means having the courage to perform your best and serve the Lord without regrets, no matter what excuses or compromises may be available. I know there are a few missionaries reading this letter who are coming down the home stretch of their missions. To you I say, never pull up, holdback, pull back, or ease up on the throttle. This should not be in your celestial makeup.

In 1972, there was an American runner named Dave Wottle who ran the 800-meters in the Munich Olympic Games. Dave was a good runner, but his trademark was his ability to finish strong. Dave had not been one of the top runners when he shocked the other runners at the US Olympic trials by winning the 800-meters and equaling the world record. Dave was unique because he ran his races in a golf cap that he had worn originally to keep his hair out of his face, but later felt that it brought him good luck. After the first 400 meters in the Olympic final, Dave was stuck in last place. He then began making his trade-mark move to finish strong, but with 100 meters remaining he was still stuck in fourth place. The distance to catch the first-place Russian runner seemed impossible. In one of the greatest Olympic finishes ever, Dave kicked his way home, passing three runners to win first place by .03 seconds over the favored Russian who had had a seemingly insur-mountable lead.[2]

Despite not being the favorite to win, Dave had been a great runner, with a powerful kick and strong lungs. He was definitely among the best in the world, and in this race he was the best finisher. His train-ing and his pattern of running had always been to finish fast. I don't know about all of the patterns in his life, but I appreciate his pattern of finishing strong. Watching the video of him cross the finish line in the Olympic finals is a powerful moment. If you were to ever video tape the final months of your mission, I hope that video would portray one powerful moment after another, ending with a tremendous finish.

In the New Testament, the Savior reminded the multitude:

> For which of you, intending to build a tower, sitteth not down first, and counteth the cost, whether he have sufficient to finish it?
>
> Lest haply, after he hath laid the foundation, and is not able to finish it, all that behold it begin to mock him,
>
> Saying, This man began to build, and was not able to finish." (Luke 14:28–30)

Elder L. Tom Perry said, "There is a real satisfaction that comes from finishing a task, especially when it is the best work we know how to do."[3] I hope that when you signed your mission papers, the cost of finishing was tallied in your mind, and that you proceeded because you knew the result would be of infinite worth.

There is a great man in my ward named Earl. He has been working with concrete for over forty years in the Arizona heat. He has the best suntan in the ward. Working with concrete is hard work and it takes

Key Missionary Moments

persistence and commitment to do it right. Earl tells me that the key to concrete is in the finishing. This means that once the concrete has been poured and is in place, for the surface to be "just right," a person needs to carefully continue to smooth and contour it until the hardness is perfect. If a person leaves their post too early, or neglects the critical nature of smoothing and finishing until the concrete is set, the concrete will never be right and will have to be redone. In Earl's words, "Anyone can pour concrete, but it takes a finisher to get it right."

I am grateful that all of you have started and are serving missions, but my gratitude will increase tenfold when I know that all of you have finished powerfully what you started so many months ago. May you complete smoothly and in a polished way what you have started. May you remember and be inspired by possibly the greatest words ever spoken on this earth when the Savior said, "It is finished" (John 19:30).

Your friend,
Brother Jeff Erickson

NOTES

1. John Cassidy, "The 2016 Masters: Jordan Spieth Gets the Yorkshire Treatment," *The New Yorker*, April 11, 2016, www.newyorker.com/news/john-cassidy/the-2016-masters-jordan-spieth-gets-the-yorkshire-treatment.
2. David Briggs, "Memories fresh of day Wottle shocked world," *The Blade*, June 24, 2012, www.toledoblade.com/sports/2012/06/24/Memories-fresh-of-day-Wottle-shocked-world.
3. L. Tom Perry, "The Joy of Honest Labor," *Ensign*, November 1986.

OPTIMISM

Dear Elders and Sisters,

My son Taft reminded me of a powerful principle when he received his midterm grades. Taft is only seven, and the only grades he has ever seen on his report card are As. He brought home his progress report one day, and my wife was reviewing it with him. He had received 87 percent on a math test and as a result, had a B on his report. My wife saw the B and said, "What happened here?" Taft saw the B and asked, "Why did I get a B?" My wife clarified that he didn't get a B for his grade, just for one test. Taft kept looking at the B, and then we could see a light in his mind turn on. Taft optimistically said, "Oh, I know what that B is for—it is for 'bonus.'"

I love missionaries with a positive attitude of faith; it seems to bring with it a spirit of hope and optimism. I love the word optimism; just hearing it makes me want to be more positive. President Gordon B. Hinckley was an optimist. He was one of those leaders who could look for and find the rainbow in every storm. He said:

> I come this evening with a plea that we stop seeking out the storms and enjoy more fully the sunlight. I'm suggesting that we accentuate the positive. I'm asking that we look a little deeper for the good, that we still our voices of insult and sarcasm, that we more generously compliment virtue and effort. . . .
>
> What I am suggesting and asking is that we turn from the negativism that so permeates our society and look for the remarkable good in the land and times in which we live, that we speak of one another's virtues more than we speak of one another's faults, that optimism replace pessimism."[1]

Being Your Best

We must always choose optimism over pessimism. Dr. John L. Lund writes that the word *sarcasm* actually comes from a Greek word "Sarkazein" meaning "to tear flesh." I think "sarcasm" is a deeply revealing word that parallels pessimism, and understanding the meaning of the word tells us how damaging pessimism can be when we have that perspective in our life.[2]

Here is how the Lord speaks of pessimism in the Doctrine and Covenants: "And that which doth not edify is not of God" (D&C 50:23). I believe that profound truth. In my life, I have been guilty of tearing others down with criticism rather than edification. I have never found satisfaction in being critical of others, but somehow, I still do it on occasion. President Faust said, "To have a simple, untroubled faith, you must keep your spiritual innocence. That requires avoiding cynicism and criticism. This is the day of the cynics, the critics, and the pickle-suckers."[3] What is a pickle-sucker? It is someone that can't seem to taste the sweetness of all that is good, virtuous, and wholesome. President Hinckley simply said, "Don't be a pickle sucker."[4] Paul said, "Whatsoever ye do, do it heartily" (Colossians 3:23). I feel that this means to do things with gusto and enthusiasm.

Years ago, on a Sunday afternoon, I was sitting at home when my wife came home from a temple recommend interview with the stake president. She had tears in her eyes; I was concerned and asked her what was wrong. It turned out they were happy tears. She shared with me that the stake president had spoken very highly about me. I was thrilled because he was a neighbor and a powerful leader who I knew had seen me at my worst. I felt grateful for a man who could somehow dwell on all that was good, holy, and virtuous in a friend and tell my wife about it. I believe she was a little surprised, but I was extremely grateful that this good man saw so much good in me. She, too, has seen my worst side on far too many occasions, but has seemed to find the best in me. I will forever be grateful for an optimistic and inspired stake president who could look past my weaknesses.

There is something great about having the spirit of optimism. You see it in your mission president, you see it in some of the local members, and you see it in the faces of great missionaries. They know that with Christ, they can conquer the world. They know that with God, anything is possible. (See Luke 1:37.) Elder Jeffrey R. Holland said, "We should honor the Savior's declaration to 'be of good cheer' [Matthew 14:27] (Indeed, it seems to me we may be more guilty of breaking that commandment than almost any other!)."[5]

Years ago, I read something memorable in a little pamphlet. This question was asked: "if someone were to pay you 10 cents for every kind word you ever spoke and collect 5 cents for every unkind word, would you be rich or poor?" I love this hypothetical question. Would we be wealthy or poor according to our outlook, disposition, and speech? President Spencer W. Kimball was a leader who was rich spiritually, mentally, and perceptually. A man once asked President Kimball, "'What do you do if you find yourself caught in a boring sacrament meeting?' President Kimball thought a moment, then replied, 'I don't know, I've never been in one.'"[6] I love that he could only see the goodness that comes from Church meetings.

I believe that when we focus on the light and the good, we see things more clearly and we begin to see as God sees. Nephi speaks of mists of darkness that were difficult to see through. With the clarity of faith, it was easy for Nephi and members of his family to see the iron rod, the tree, and the fountain.

Part of optimism is seeing people as God sees them. As a missionary, we must see the people we teach as the precious children of God that they are. Do we see the good and the godlike potential in them, or do we get caught up in the muddy waters of doubt and pessimism? I believe in a God who looks for opportunities to bless, rather than chances to punish. I believe that He is so merciful because He focuses on what's ahead, rather than the darkness in the past. I believe He sees so much good in His children.

Here is a little poem that demonstrates a clear and optimistic perspective:

> We have the nicest garbage man.
> He empties out our garbage can.
> He's just as nice as he can be.
> He always stops and talks with me.
> My mother says she doesn't like his smell,
> But, then, she doesn't know him very well.[7]

The eternal optimist President Hinckley said,

I [am] an optimist concerning the work of the Lord. I cannot believe that God has established His work in the earth to have it fail. I cannot believe that it is getting weaker. I know that it is getting stronger. . . .

I have a simple and solemn faith that right will triumph and that truth will prevail. I am not so naive as to believe there will not be setbacks, but I believe that "truth crushed to earth will rise again."[8]

The greatest people that you know or will ever know are optimists. The Savior was the ultimate optimist. May you and I follow Him and be optimists in our lives, and may we find the rainbow in every storm.

Your friend,
Brother Jeff Erickson

NOTES

1.   Gordon B. Hinckley, "The Lord Is at the Helm," *BYU Speeches*, March 6, 1994.

2.   John L. Lund, *For All Eternity: A Four-Talk Set to Strengthen Your Marriage* (Covenant, 2003), audio CD.

3.   James E. Faust, "An Untroubled Faith," *Ensign*, March 1988.

4.   Gordon B. Hinckley, "Let Not Your Heart Be Troubled," *BYU Speeches*, October 29, 1974.)

5.   Jeffrey R. Holland, "The Tongue of Angels," *Ensign*, May 2007.

6.   A. Roger Merrill, "To Be Edified and Rejoice Together," *Ensign*, January 2007.

7.   Quoted in Vaughn J. Featherstone, "To Walk in High Places," *New Era*, October 1979.

8.   Gordon B. Hinckley, "Words of the Prophet: The Spirit of Optimism," *New Era*, July 2001.

GRATITUDE

Dear Elders and Sisters,

Many years ago, I was at an amusement park with my family waiting in a line. My then four-year-old son Tanner was eating an orange while waiting, and he shared a piece with me. I ate the piece of orange, and we continued to move forward in the line. A few moments later, he said to me, "What do you say?" I responded, "Huh?" He said again, "What do you say?" I recognized what he was doing and said, "Oh, thanks, buddy." His response, "No problem, Dad." Here was a young boy reminding his father of the importance of gratitude.

There are many examples of gratitude in the Book of Mormon. Captain Moroni was "a man whose heart did swell with thanksgiving" (Alma 48:12). Amulek said we should "live in thanksgiving daily" (Alma 34:38). Alma said, "Let thy heart be full of thanks" (Alma 37:37).

Lehi demonstrates one of the greatest examples of gratitude in all scripture. Lehi spent much of his life laboring to provide for his family, and he had been blessed and prospered financially. Then the Lord came and asked him to leave nearly every worldly possession he had, and Lehi obeyed with "exactness" (Alma 57:21). He left all his possessions and the comforts of his home that he had spent years building. He took his family, and they departed into the wilderness. Three days into the wilderness, Lehi stopped his family and built an altar to give thanks. (See 1 Nephi 2:1–7.) Why does Nephi record that detail? Maybe he was inspired to do so. Maybe it was just an impressive lesson in gratitude. Whatever the reason, I am grateful for Lehi, who understood that life is not about what we think we need, but rather what Heavenly Father knows we need.

As a missionary, do you live in thanksgiving daily? What do you express gratitude for?

A good companion?
A good lesson?
A good investigator?
A good day?
A good mission president?
A good ward or branch?
A good zone leader?
A good answered prayer?
A good morning of scripture study?

What about gratitude for being around great missionaries, teaching a powerful Spirit-filled lesson, or witnessing the Spirit change someone's heart? Or having gratitude for hearing someone say "yes" to a baptismal invitation, bringing someone back into activity, learning a foreign language in a short period of time, or finding someone to teach through yet another miracle? There are so many things to be grateful for as a missionary. I hope you are expressing your gratitude to our Heavenly Father immediately and often.

I read or heard somewhere that you will learn to be more grateful by writing a daily thank-you note. I believe that, as a missionary, writing a weekly letter of gratitude (more appropriate than doing it daily) would help you develop further the spirit of gratitude. When my daughter Holland was eighteen months old, one of the first words she learned was "thank you." We would do well to follow her pattern of learning and make gratitude one of the first lessons we master. "Cicero, the ancient Roman statesman, called gratitude 'the mother of virtues.'"[1] I believe if we can learn the critical principle of gratitude, other wonderful attributes will follow.

Here is a promise to the thankful: "And he who receiveth all things with thankfulness shall be made glorious" (D&C 78:19). What does it mean to be made glorious? It means to be made magnificent, wonderful, splendid, brilliant, beautiful, and exceptional in the eyes of the Lord. As a missionary, your life will be blessed by following Alma's counsel: "And when thou risest in the morning let thy heart be full of thanks unto God" (Alma 37:37). If you savor the blessings of God and desire to have an abundance of His love, here are three verses that will help you increase those blessings:

1. "Thou shalt thank the Lord thy God in all things" (D&C 59:7)
2. "[Do] all things with prayer and thanksgiving" (D&C 46:7)
3. "Always [return] thanks unto God for whatsoever things ye do receive" (Alma 7:23)

The Savior in 3 Nephi demonstrates a powerful example of gratitude. The Savior had left the Nephites and promised to return the next day. When he returned, he found his newly called disciples teaching the people what he had taught, praying for the Holy Ghost, and baptizing. He witnessed that the Holy Ghost had fallen upon them. When he saw that they were filled with the Holy Ghost and with fire, he taught them to immediately pray and give thanks.

> And it came to pass that Jesus departed out of the midst of them, and went a little way off from them and bowed himself to the earth, and he said:
>
> Father, I thank thee that thou hast given the Holy Ghost unto these whom I have chosen; and it is because of their belief in me that I have chosen them out of the world. (3 Nephi 19:19–20)

I am impressed with how quickly the Savior was able to recognize and show gratitude for the sacred blessings that come from God.

The people of Alma, despite much adversity, were full of gratitude. They rejoiced in the Lord's tender mercies as "they poured out their thanks to God because he had been merciful unto them" (Mosiah 24:21). I believe missions are the same way; you can focus on the adversity and difficulty, or be grateful for the many tender mercies you see and feel on a daily basis.

Near the end of my mission, the unforgettable Robert and Carolyn White family had been baptized. They had four boys, three of which were baptized at the time, while the youngest was not old enough yet. My companion and I had been very close to them and had been blessed to watch the hand of the Lord change their lives and grow their testimonies. About a year after I returned from my mission, I vividly remember a sacred event where I poured out my thanks to God for a tremendous tender mercy he granted to me. I had received a phone call from Robert White in Nova Scotia, Canada, inviting me to their family's temple sealing in Washington, D.C. I was thrilled to hear they were being sealed and made arrangements to fly from Utah for the sacred occasion. I was sitting in a sealing room of the Washington D.C. temple, when in walked Robert and Carolyn White. The Spirit filled my soul as this wonderful couple knelt at the altar and were sealed for eternity. Leaving an impression I will never forget, after the marriage, in marched the four White boys. They looked angelic all dressed in white as they entered the sealing room. The boys and the parents all knelt at the altar and were sealed as a family. I sat in that sacred sealing room that day basking in the Spirit of God with tears in my eyes, and my gratitude cup completely overflowing. I was so grateful for a loving Father to allow me to witness, and be a part of, the White family's journey toward the kingdom of God.

May you do as the prophet Alma suggests and "give thanks in all things" (Mosiah 26:39). May you feel the blessings of gratitude impact your mission for the better.

Your friend,
Brother Jeff Erickson

NOTES

1.   Cicero quoted in Sterling W. Sill, *The Law of the Harvest* (Salt Lake City: Bookcraft, 1963), 117.

HABITS

Dear Elders and Sisters,

A few years ago, I was working in my dental office when I heard the thunderous crash of an automobile accident outside. It sounded very close, so I rushed outside to see what had happened. A school bus had crashed into a small white car, collapsing the driver's side of the car. There were two ladies in the car on their way to pick up one of their children at school. I looked at the two ladies, and they were hurt, it didn't seem life-threatening, but there was blood and moaning. The driver's leg was badly damaged due to the collapsed door on her side. I have been trained in emergency medicine and was the first person on the scene.

In this situation, as someone trained in emergency medicine, there are specific things I should do: call 911, assess injuries, and perform CPR as necessary. As a dentist, the first thing I did as I opened the door to assess the injuries was check the driver's teeth. In my shock, I reverted back to my habits. I lifted her upper and lower lips to evaluate her teeth. I finally came to my senses and began to assess the other injuries as someone called 911, and my assistant came out with gloves and offered support and help. I was grateful the injuries were not life-threatening, and I learned a valuable lesson in how powerful habits can be.

Good and bad habits can become automatic. A missionary getting out of bed on time each day is a sign of a good habit. A missionary following the missionary study plan is a good habit. A missionary dropping to his or her knees everyday represents a good habit. A missionary extending invitations every time he or she feels the Spirit is a good habit. A missionary going to bed on time is a good habit.

Good habits are the essence of good missionaries. May you create habits and routines in your missionary lifestyle that are righteous. Benjamin Franklin warned, "Tis easier to prevent bad habits than to break them."[1]

A scriptural word for *habit* is "pattern." The Lord is a God of perfect order and operates in consistent habits and patterns. His patterns are always perfectly consistent with His principles and His approach to His children. He said, "And again, I will give unto you a *pattern in all things*, that ye may not be deceived" (D&C 52:14; emphasis added).

It has been said that practice makes perfect. I would like to modify that and say that *practice produces.* We produce according to how we practice. We become a product of our life practices. If we have righteous habits, we become righteous. If we practice wickedness, we become a wicked product. The beauty of the plan is that we will produce what we plant and grow. We will not produce a sinful product through righteous living. Conversely, we will not produce a righteous product through sinful actions. We will simply produce according to our daily habits. Alma said, "Therefore, if a man bringeth forth good works he hearkeneth unto the voice of the good shepherd, and he doth follow him; but whosoever bringeth forth evil works, the same becometh a child of the devil, for he hearkeneth unto his voice, and doth follow him" (Alma 5:41). Elder Faust said, "Each new day that dawns can be a new day for us to begin to change. We can change our environment. We can change our lives by substituting new habits for old. We can mold our character and future by purer thoughts and nobler actions."[2]

A few years ago, a young wife was struggling with her husband's habits and was tired of being ignored. She felt that he was obsessed with playing video games most of the day. She ran an advertisement on Craigslist. Among other things, she posted: "One husband to the highest bidder." The ad describes her husband as "easy to maintain, just feed and water every 3–5 hours." The ad also warned purchasers that they would need "internet service and space for gaming." The ad noted that she was willing to "trade her husband of two years for an acceptable replacement." One response she received was an offer to trade him for a blue bag of skittles.[3] The ad was placed in fun, but it also reveals that a young wife wasn't happy about some of her husband's habits and their undesirable results.

There is a Spanish proverb that reads: "Habits are at first cobwebs, then cables." This proverb is a great voice of warning to us as missionaries telling us that everything we do matters. C. A. Hill said, "We sow our thoughts, and we reap our actions; we sow our actions, and we reap our habits; we sow our habits, and we reap our characters; we sow our characters, and we reap our destiny."[4] We can truly say that the habits of a missionary determine the destiny of a missionary.

Elder Dellenbach said, "Research indicates it takes 21 days to overcome a habit, so why not avoid swearing for 21 days?"[5] With that mindset, is there anything righteous we can't do for twenty-one days? Missionaries can develop, with the strength of God, a variety of wonderful habits with discipline and the Atonement of Jesus Christ. May your habits be an extension of your righteous desires and attributes. May you operate your life as the Lord would, and in twenty-one days say, "Behold, mine house is a house of order" (D&C 132:8).

Your friend,
Brother Jeff Erickson

Being Your Best

NOTES

1.   Benjamin Franklin, *Poor Richard's Almanack* (The Peter Pauper Press, 1981).

2.   James E. Faust, "The Power to Change," *Ensign*, November 2007.)

3.   "Logan woman posts husband for sale on Craigslist," *The Sale Lake Tribune*, November 21, 2011, archive.sltrib.com/story.php?ref=/sltrib/news/52956974-78 /game-alyse-baddley-husband.html.csp.

4.   Burton Stevenson, comp., *The Home Book of Quotations*, 6th ed. (New York: Dodd, Mead & Company, 1949), 845.

5.   Robert K. Dellenbach, "Profanity," *New Era*, May 1992.

PERFECTION PENDING

Dear Elders and Sisters,

I remember one hot summer day a few years ago we had a pick-up soccer game at the park. I was designated goalie because it was only young kids playing. Tanner, one of my very competitive sons, was on my team. He ran back to me in the goal box at the beginning of the game and said, "Dad, don't disappoint me." I remember a few shots going past me that day, but I also made some great saves. Tanner's words were not only humorous and thought-provoking, but also motivating and inspiring for me. I was never discouraged by his remarks. I believe Heavenly Father would echo the same sentiment to us, "Don't disappoint me," knowing that we will fail nearly as many times as we succeed. He will rejoice in our successes and lift us in our failures.

A loving Heavenly Father has given us wonderful counsel on how we can approach life and missions: "For we know that it is by grace that we are saved, after all we can do" (2 Nephi 25:23). The grace in this equation is indispensable—if we eliminate grace, we cannot be saved. I must remind you that in this dispensation, there has never been or ever will be a perfect missionary. There will be thousands of wonderful missionaries who work hard and serve faithfully, but none will be without sin. May you strive to be saved by grace and acknowledge that, despite your best efforts, they will not be enough.

Elder Holland said, "So be kind regarding human frailty—your own as well as that of those who serve with you in a Church led by volunteer, mortal men and women. Except in the case of His only perfect Begotten Son, imperfect people are all God has ever had to work with. That must be terribly frustrating to Him, but He deals with it. So should we."[1]

The above quote is loaded, so I will first focus on human frailty. In the New Testament, John profoundly stated, "If we say that we have no sin, we deceive ourselves, and the truth is not in us" (1 John 1:8). We all sin, make mistakes, fall short, and have human frailties. Every missionary struggles with not being perfect. God recognizes this and would never have you beat yourself down because of it. God is a God of mercy and discipline. He will never focus on our shortcomings, but will always focus on our efforts and successes. Why should we be different than a merciful God?

Before we came to this earth, God knew we would struggle and fall short of what we wanted to do and become. For this purpose, there was a merciful Atonement prepared for us to fill in every possible gap, weakness, shortcoming, and sin. The existence of the Atonement tells us that God knew we would never be perfect, and that every child of God would need a Savior. For this reason, we can shout and declare that the Atonement is amazing, remarkable, wonderful, marvelous, divine, and truly miraculous.

The second phrase of Elder Holland's quote teaches us that God works with imperfect people, deals with it, and so should we. First, we need to deal with our own imperfections. We need to know that as missionaries our local bishops and stake presidents aren't perfect, our companions aren't perfect, our parents aren't perfect, and our mission presidents aren't perfect, but neither are we. We are all striving to become perfect, but we are not even close yet. We can't be weighed down with our imperfections. We are here to spend years refining our characteristics and attributes. We must learn to deal effectively with those nagging shortcomings of the natural man. Elder Nelson stated, "My heart goes out to conscientious Saints who, because of their shortcomings, allow feelings of depression to rob them of happiness in life."[2]

King Benjamin said, "And see that all these things are done in wisdom and order; for it is not requisite that a man should run faster than he has strength. And again, it is expedient that he should be diligent, that thereby he might win the prize; therefore, all things must be done in order" (Mosiah 4:27). Please don't be depressed because you continue to show a lack of patience. There's no use in becoming discouraged because you don't speak the language as well as your companion. A loving Heavenly Father does not want you to be overcome

35

with despair because you were afraid to challenge an investigator at the opportune time. We learn from our struggles, and we operate as directed "in wisdom and order."

Every missionary might do well to follow my young son's example. One fast Sunday, when I was interviewing my three-year-old Taft, I asked him a series of questions. One of the questions was: "What is the best thing about Taft?" He said, "I love myself." There is wisdom in his words. Despite falling short, having many imperfections, lacking all of the talents we desire, and still making mistakes, we all need to have confidence that we are children of a loving Father. We have great value! If God loves us, why shouldn't we also love ourselves?

Here are some important reminders to remember along our very long and slow pathway to perfection. "We all need to remember: men are that they might have joy—not guilt trips!"[3] If we do the best we can, the Lord will bless us according to our deeds and the desires of our hearts. (See D&C 137:9.) "Wherefore, continue in patience until ye are perfected" (D&C 67:13). These last two thoughts are gentle, yet powerful, reminders that perfection is a process and won't be achieved in the next eighteen months or two years.

If you can remember Elder Nelson's three-word phrase you will remember to serve and progress in your mission one day at a time. He said, "Perfection is pending."[4] I pray that your heart will be filled with love and joy as you contemplate that your perfection is pending.

Your friend,
Brother Jeff Erickson

NOTES

1. Jeffrey R. Holland, "'Lord, I Believe,'" *Ensign*, November 2013.
2. Russell M. Nelson, "Perfection Pending," *Ensign*, November 1995.
3. Ibid.
4. Ibid.

KEEP A RECORD

Dear Elders and Sisters,

Two years ago, a man walked into my office (I was the bishop at the time), and he was discouraged and struggling. He was a good man with the weight of the world on his shoulders. We counseled together for a while, and then I asked if I could give him a priesthood blessing. He agreed, and in the blessing the Lord reminded him of his potential and destiny, and that He would strengthen him in his time of trial. The blessing was just what this good brother needed to continue on the right path and believe he could succeed. We had a tremendous experience together that day. Commitments were made and a plan was put in place as he left the office.

Since that visit to the bishop's office, I have watched this good brother and his family make wonderful steps forward. I had completely forgotten about this sacred experience until recently when I was reading some pages in my journal.

Elder Henry B. Eyring shared these thoughts:

> When our children were very small, I started to write down a few things about what happened every day. Let me tell you how that got started. I came home late from a Church assignment. It was after dark. My father-in-law, who lived near us, surprised me as I walked toward the front door of my house. He was carrying a load of pipes over his shoulder, walking very fast and dressed in his work clothes. I knew that he had been building a system to pump water from a stream below us up to our property.
>
> He smiled, spoke softly, and then rushed past me into the darkness to go on with his work. I took a few steps toward the house, thinking of what he was doing for us, and just as I got to the door, I heard in my

mind—not in my own voice—these words: "I'm not giving you these experiences for yourself. Write them down."

I went inside. I didn't go to bed. Although I was tired, I took out some paper and began to write. And as I did, I understood the message I had heard in my mind. I was supposed to record for my children to read, someday in the future, how I had seen the hand of God blessing our family. Grandpa didn't have to do what he was doing for us. He could have had someone else do it or not have done it at all. But he was serving us, his family, in the way covenant disciples of Jesus Christ always do. I knew that was true. And so I wrote it down, so that my children could have the memory someday when they would need it."[1]

I believe one of the Lord's great training grounds is the mission, possibly even the greatest training ground of our lifetime. Being tutored of the Lord is an amazing experience—sometimes difficult, but always enlightening. While we are being trained as missionaries, it is critical to record many of the principles and lessons learned. If we don't record them, many of them will be forgotten, and some will have to be relearned. I have noticed in my life that relearning certain lessons can be a painful process. My purpose today is to plead with you to keep a record of your mission.

Here is what Alma said to his son Helaman at the close of his life, "And I also command you that ye keep a record of this people, according as I have done, upon the plates of Nephi, and keep all these things sacred which I have kept, even as I have kept them; for it is for a wise purpose that they are kept" (Alma 37:2). There is great insight in the phrase "for a wise purpose." The things we write may be for us or for our posterity, but be sure that whomever it is for, "it is for a wise purpose." There is great wisdom in recording sacred things. There will be sacred experiences, life lessons, sacred spiritual instruction, and direct answers to prayers. We must record these things, as it will certainly bless us, as well as others, in the future.

What should you record? "But behold, there are many books and many records of every kind, and they have been kept chiefly by the Nephites" (Helaman 3:15). I am sure the records of every kind were historical, spiritual, and some very personal. Here are some of my thoughts on what you should record as a missionary. I hope as you read the scriptures, you are recording verses, phrases, and words that the Spirit prompts you to remember and record. I hope you are keeping the scripture journal you have been asked to keep. "And after this manner we keep the records, for it is according to the commandments of our fathers" (Omni 1:9).

In your regular journal, I would have sections: "lessons learned," "principles learned," "sacred experiences," "humorous experiences," "times when I felt the hand of the Lord," and any other categories you think would be a blessing to record. You can record talks, blessings, amazing lessons, counsel from a wise mission president, zone conference highlights, precious investigator comments, and any other Spirit-filled thoughts, impressions, and comments.

These experiences you are having will change you, but time causes us to forget how penetrating they were in the moment, so you must record them. I am grateful that I have recorded so many experiences I have had. I have recorded great things my kids have done, humorous quotes from each of my children, great experiences we have had as a family, and numerous spiritual insights I have learned from the Spirit. I have a file called "Jeff's Sacred Experiences," and I attempt, like President Eyring, to record at least one weekly experience where I see the hand of God in my life. It has not been very difficult to recall and record one weekly sacred experience.

President Kimball said, "By now, in my own personal history, I have managed to fill seventy-eight large volumes which are my personal journal. There have been times when I have been so tired at the end of a day that the effort could hardly be managed, but I am so grateful that I have not let slip away from me and my posterity those things which needed to be recorded."[2]

As I have read books and scriptures or heard talks or lessons, I have recorded impressions and stories. I now have numerous talks recorded and thousands of pages of stories, quotes, and thoughts under a variety of topics. I have written articles and parables and saved precious promptings. I love to review some of those things as I prepare for talks or presentations. My regret is that my recording wasn't very organized as a missionary. I do believe it is still far better to record than to be overwhelmed by organization. I would encourage you to organize your thoughts and journals now, so you can use them for talks when you come home and for reviewing things that are important to you later.

Critical Missionary Advice

You will cherish being able to quickly find times where you felt the Spirit or felt the hand of God. You will be grateful to have a list of very sacred experiences. Doing this now will be a blessing to you in the future.

I hope you will record talks, quotes, poems, scriptures, parallels, object lessons, stories, personal experiences, and funny experiences. All of these will be worth sharing at one point or another in your life. You will draw on your mission memories for the rest of eternity. "Wherefore, the things which are pleasing unto the world I do not write, but the things which are pleasing unto God and unto those who are not of the world" (1 Nephi 6:5.)

Let me share one experience I recorded about my daughter Holland that always brings a smile to my face. We were just finishing Sunday dinner when four-year-old Holland moved over to sit by me. For dinner we had had barbecue ribs. She had been in time-out for some reason and was now back at the table. While sitting by me, she spilled something on the sleeve of my white shirt, but I hadn't noticed because we were all talking as a family. Holland ran to a drawer and grabbed a white dishcloth and began to wipe away at the spill on my sleeve. After she began scrubbing harder and harder, I finally looked to see what she was doing. Nearly my entire right arm, from shoulder to sleeve, was covered with barbecue sauce. I looked at the shirt, and then I stared at her. I looked back at the shirt and back at her one more time. I really wasn't mad, but didn't know if I should laugh or be upset. She then looked at me and perceiving my response to be negative, she said, "I think I will just go back to my room." For me, it was a humorous and memorable moment that I'm grateful I recorded so I can always remember.

When the Savior came to the Nephites, He powerfully taught how important sacred records were: "And it came to pass that he said unto Nephi: Bring forth the record which ye have kept" (3 Nephi 23:7). The day may come when the Savior asks us to do the same thing. I pray that our record may be pleasing unto Him, and that we personally may be able to testify that our personal record was for "a wise purpose."

Your friend,
Brother Jeff Erickson

Critical Missionary Advice

40

NOTES

1. Henry B. Eyring, "O Remember, Remember," *Ensign*, November 2007.
2. JoAnn Jolley, "News of the Church," *Ensign*, October 1980.

Critical Missionary Advice

DISTRACTIONS

Dear Elders and Sisters,

During my first year of dental school, I drove a sports car to school every day. The final section of the road on the way to school had numerous curves that wound up the final hill to the school. I found the twisting road very exhilarating to drive. The road had about ten turns on it in the space of one mile. I drove this road twice every weekday for nine months. On the last time down the hill before my summer break, there was a light rain falling. I was in a rush to be somewhere and was traveling faster than I should have been. For the first time in nine months as I raced my car down the hill, I heard the Holy Ghost say, "Slow down." I hate to admit this, but I was distracted by the excitement of the downhill drive. The car was moving faster and faster, and the turns were entertaining. I continued my descent down the windy road, and for the second time, I heard, "Slow down." Still very distracted, I continued down the hill moving faster and faster. The Holy Ghost spoke to me a third time, and I again ignored the warnings of the Spirit.

The last turn on the hill is a hairpin fifteen mile-per-hour turn. I hit this final tight turn going way too fast, especially since the road was a little bit wet. On the wet asphalt, my car began to slide into the opposite lane. Unfortunately, there was a car coming in the opposite direction, and I hit this vehicle nearly head-on after I had entered into the turn. The force of the accident was both abrupt and intense. Fortunately for me, neither myself nor the other driver was severely hurt, but we both suffered some minor injuries. My car was totaled, and I never drove that road again in a sports car, despite having three more years at the school. I have often asked myself why I didn't just listen to the Spirit. The answer is that it was a moment of being distracted by other things. It was an accident and a lesson that I will never forget.

One of the great stories of the Old Testament is the story of Nehemiah, who felt compelled to rebuild the walls of Jerusalem. He resigned from his labors as cupbearer to the king and went to serve the Lord rebuilding Jerusalem. "And they said, Let us rise up and build. So they strengthened their hands for this good work" (Nehemiah 2:18). He was going about the Lord's business, and he was doing a great work rebuilding the walls and gates of Jerusalem, yet he had his detractors.

> Now it came to pass, when Sanballat, and Tobiah, and Geshem the Arabian, and the rest of our enemies, heard that I had builded the wall, and that there was no breach left therein; (though at that time I had not set up the doors upon the gates;)
>
> That Sanballat and Geshem sent unto me, saying, Come let us meet together in some one of the villages in the plain of Ono. But they thought to do me mischief. (Nehemiah 6:1–2)

He said, "And I sent messengers unto them, saying, I am doing a great work, so that I cannot come down: why should the work cease, whilst I leave it, and come down to you?" (Nehemiah 6:3). They continued to persist in distracting Nehemiah—five times— but he could not and would not be deterred. They put fear into the hearts of Nehemiah's people, but he prayed, "Now therefore, O God, strengthen my hands" (Nehemiah 6:9). Nehemiah was focused on "a great work" and would not be deterred by other influences.

Nehemiah's faith and persistence in doing "great things" paid off because "the wall was finished in the twenty and fifth day of the month" (Nehemiah 6:15). "And it came to pass, that when all our enemies heard thereof, and all the heathen that were about us saw these things, they were much cast down in their own eyes: for they perceived that this work was wrought of our God" (Nehemiah 6:16). When the adversary sees a missionary who cannot be distracted, he is cast down, because he knows that that elder or sister is performing a "work wrought of God." Distractions can take the best missionary and make him average. They can also take a good missionary and make him below average. Beware of distractions; they may come in numerous forms in the mission field. Distractions for missionaries can waste precious time while minimizing your effectiveness as a missionary and the overall sacredness of your experience. They can cause you to forget the importance of "always remembering" whom you serve.

Synonyms for the word *distraction* include, diversion, interruption, interference, or disturbance.[1] These synonyms powerfully describe how devastating distractions can be to furthering the work of the Lord. If a missionary is distracted by a weekly letter or a communication from a girlfriend or boyfriend back home, it can disturb the work. If a missionary is looking for ways to do the easiest things, they are interfering with what the Spirit could really do to further the work. What about when a missionary settles into a feeling of laziness, or when they know they could be much more productive? Truly, this must be interfering with the work of God.

Here are a few distractions to beware of as a full-time missionary:

- Wasting time
- Doing the things that are the least productive
- Focusing too much time on leadership responsibilities rather than proselyting
- Not getting back to interested people in a timely fashion
- Using the members ineffectively rather than effectively
- Being social with people instead of being instruments and missionaries
- Making p-day your most important day of the week
- Flirting with missionaries of the opposite sex
- Writing inappropriate letters to members of the opposite sex back home
- Spending time worrying about relationships back at home
- Being content with not doing your best
- Slacking in obedience because those around you are less obedient
- Not being fully committed to the work

Critical Missionary Advice

During my full-time mission service in Canada, I had the chance to go on splits with numerous missionaries. Splits were always a blessing and a great learning experience. They were a good get-to-know-you experience with missionaries whom I didn't know very well. I remember one exchange where I did splits with an elder who was one of the most difficult missionaries in our mission. I spent the day with him and we had some great experiences, and met many potential investigators that day. I learned many things that day, but two specific things that have stayed with me through the years.

First, this missionary might have been the most talented, and most personable missionary in our entire mission. He was good with people and was fearless in talking to them. He was clever, fun, and witty. Second, this missionary was completely distracted. He boasted that he spent numerous nights on the phone with his girlfriend back home; he told me his monthly bill was in the six-hundred-dollar range (this was the days before cheap long-distance cell coverage). The mission president was aware of these distractions, and was doing all he could to encourage this missionary to stop and to keep him on a mission. The result of these distractions in this missionary's life was a disappointing mission with little change in his character, little success, and a minimal positive impact on the lives of those he met. In many instances, he was able to take quality companions and good missionaries and distract them from being fully engaged in the work of the Lord.

Elder Dallin H. Oaks said, "The number of good things we can do far exceeds the time available to accomplish them. Some things are better than good, and these are the things that should command priority attention in our lives."[2] As missionaries, the better and best things should occupy our efforts during the precious time that we have during our full-time service. Some missionaries get distracted by good things such as too much service time, while neglecting more important teaching opportunities. I remember a group of missionaries in my mission who spent much of their time baking cookies, writing in their journals excessively, and spending an inordinate amount of time planning in their apartment. While all of these things were probably good, there were better things they could have been doing to further the work. Their success and teaching skills were extremely limited as they were not out finding and teaching.

"As we consider various choices, we should remember that it is not enough that something is good. Other choices are better, and still others are best. Even though a particular choice is more costly, its far greater value may make it the best choice of all."[3] We have critical choices to make about how we most effectively use our proselyting time. May we use inspiration and the Spirit of the Lord to do the things that will bring about the most good and will please the Lord.

The prophet Nehemiah can be a great example to us since there are numerous potential distractions, but we are doing a great work. Let us ask the Lord to strengthen our hands and minds so we may persist without distraction in performing these great missionary labors. Let us thrust in our sickle with all our might, and bring salvation to our souls. (See D&C 4:4.) May you not be distracted as you "magnify the calling whereunto I have called you, and the mission with which I have commissioned you" (D&C 88:80). Be focused.

Your friend,
Brother Jeff Erikson

Critical Missionary Advice

NOTES

1.   *Thesaurus.com*, s.v "distraction," accessed February 27, 2017, www.thesaurus.com/browse/distraction.
2.   Dallin H. Oaks, "Good, Better, Best," *Ensign*, November 2007.
3.   Ibid.

NOT OF THE WORLD

Dear Elders and Sisters,

In the New Testament, we read, "Love not the world, neither the things that are in the world. If any man love the world, the love of the Father is not in him" (1 John 2:15). For missionaries, one of the challenges you face is to give up the world for eighteen months or two years. I pray you accept this challenge and love not those things that you should be giving up while you serve the Lord. In our day, a good part of letting go of the world lies in giving up social media back home in Babylon while serving afar.

I hear stories of missionaries violating mission rules in numerous ways as they cannot let go of the world and continue to spend the Lord's time on social media sites such as Facebook, Twitter, Snapchat, etc. There are even those who spend time on inappropriate internet sites, and some spend their email time surfing the Internet. These are all things the Lord asked you to forsake during your sacred time of service. The Lord said, "For it is better that ye should deny yourselves of these things, wherein ye will take up your cross, than that ye should be cast into hell" (3 Nephi 12:30).

There is a lesson for missionaries found in the experience of a young girl named Alexa. She was a high school sophomore who was walking along Victory Boulevard on Staten Island one evening. She was texting and walking, not watching where she was going. Suddenly, she plunged downward into a smelly pit. She fell into an open manhole without warning and landed in the abyss of raw sewage.[1] When missionaries are not paying attention to the mission rules of technology, like Alexa, they can be exposed to the sewage of the world. There is plenty of filth available that will suddenly confront missionaries when they are not carefully observing the mission guidelines. Many missionaries will justify their inappropriate media actions, but beware, because you never know where those steps of disobedience will end up.

If a missionary is unable to let go of social media, Facebook friends, inappropriate conversations via email, texting, or any other form of Babylonian baggage from afar, how can they ever forsake the things of the world? Remember, the Lord said, "Behold, I, the Lord, who was crucified for the sins of the world, give unto you a commandment that you shall forsake the world" (D&C 53:2). One of the reasons you are sent on a mission is to change permanently, not just for the time of your mission service. Part of that "mighty change" is giving up any form of addiction or need to keep up with the world back home. Of course, it is appropriate to communicate with parents, family, and close friends through email, but there are lines that missionaries must be careful not to cross.

I am aware that certain missions are using some social media, iPads, and computers for proselyting and other limited uses; those elders and sisters must take special precautions to not misuse these tools. If you have had a problem with social media and websites in the past, watch yourself, and even inform your mission president if necessary so you can obtain the appropriate help.

I know of a returned missionary who has been home from his mission for just a few months and struggles with online gaming. Part of his meager income is spent on a nightly internet video game commitment. He has chosen to miss some church and family functions and other important events to fulfill his nightly gaming commitment. I am not certain how gaming blesses his life each night, but I have concluded that this young man has been unable to let go of the world. I would suspect that while he attempted to serve the Lord for two years as a missionary, he violated many of the computer mission guidelines. Why would someone who loves God more than the world allow a video game to govern their daily activities?

President Kimball shared this powerful story years ago:

> I am reminded of an article I read some years ago about a group of men who had gone to the jungles to capture monkeys. They tried a number of different things to catch the monkeys, including nets. But finding that the nets could injure such small creatures, they finally came upon

Critical Missionary Advice

an ingenious solution. They built a large number of small boxes, and in the top of each they bored a hole just large enough for a monkey to get his hand into. They then set these boxes out under the trees and in each one they put a nut that the monkeys were particularly fond of.

When the men left, the monkeys began to come down from the trees and examine the boxes. Finding that there were nuts to be had, they reached into the boxes to get them. But when a monkey would try to withdraw his hand with the nut, he could not get his hand out of the box because his little fist, with the nut inside, was now too large.

At about this time, the men would come out of the underbrush and converge on the monkeys. And here is the curious thing: When the monkeys saw the men coming, they would shriek and scramble about with the thought of escaping; but as easy as it would have been, they would not let go of the nut so that they could withdraw their hands from the boxes and thus escape. The men captured them easily.[2]

What about us as missionaries? What are those things we are hanging onto that hold us captive to the world and its traps? Unlike the monkeys, may we see the danger of not letting go and choose to free ourselves from the world by simply letting go and freeing ourselves from a computer and a social media world and its potentially damaging effects. The Savior said, "As long as I am in the world, I am the light of the world" (John 9:5). May we emulate the Savior, and, as long as we are in the world, be a light unto the world. The greatest compliment the Savior could offer any missionary is what he said of His disciples: "They are not of the world, even as I am not of the world" (John 17:16).

Your friend,
Brother Jeff Erickson

Critical Missionary Advice

NOTES

1. Dan Childs, Dean Praetorius, and ABC News Medical Unit, "Watch Out! Texting While Walking Lands Teen in Trouble," *ABC News*, July 14, 2009.
2. Spencer W. Kimball, "The False Gods We Worship," *Ensign*, June 1976.

CONVENIENT COMMANDMENTS

Critical Missionary
Advice

Dear Elders and Sisters,

A few years ago, the BYU women's rugby team was playing in the post-season tournament. They had just won a big game against Wisconsin-Milwaukee overpowering them 46–7. In the next round, they would be playing Penn State. They had worked hard all year and had performed well. The game against Penn State was scheduled to be held on a Sunday. Alternatives were pursued, but none were found. The decision was made by these devoted young ladies to forfeit the playoff game, thus eliminating them from a shot at the championship. The club team was not actually sponsored by BYU, and, technically, they could have still played. The most impressive part of their decision was that it was not made by the coach or one key player. The team held a vote and the players unanimously decided not to play on Sunday.[1]

I want to share a few thoughts on convenient and inconvenient commandments. The convenient ones appear to be pretty easy to keep. As a missionary, convenient commandments might be reading your scriptures and saying your prayers every day. It may be getting up and out the door on time. For many missionaries, these commandments are pretty convenient and easy. For a member of the Church who has an active family, it may be easy to attend Church with their family each week. It is easy to live the Word of Wisdom when people all around you are living it. It is easy to be honest when there is no penalty for honesty. It is easy to honor your mother and father when they are great and agree with you. It is easy to have family night when your parents make you be there. There are many commandments that in many instances are very convenient, and, in our present environments, very easy to live. Do you still get blessed for living these commandments? Absolutely. Follow along, though, for a more powerful plea and insight.

What changes occur in our decision-making process when we are faced with some inconvenient commandments? What are inconvenient commandments? These are the ones that are tempting enough to break. They are the ones that aren't second nature, or aren't easily followed. They are the commandments where you feel you can justify your disobedient behavior. They are the ones where you feel like you have legitimate excuses to violate these more inconvenient commandments. They are the ones where we need to step up, as Latter-day Saints, and show God we love Him at all costs.

Inconvenient commandments are the ones where you have to stretch your faith to be faithful and obey. They are the ones that seem to come at such inopportune times. It is easy to keep the Sabbath day holy until the Super Bowl comes around; then, somehow, we forget the Sabbath and remember football. It is easy keep the commandment of being kind until someone is mean to you. It is easy to love the people of your mission until one is rude and belligerent. It is easy to be honest unless the consequences are big. It is easy to pay tithing until you don't have enough money to pay for your other commitments. It is easy to stay away from pornography until you are alone on a computer or cell phone, and the adversary says, "No one will ever know."

Frequently, in life we model behaviors that say, "Just this one time is okay. It's not that big of a deal to not get up on time or leave the apartment on time." It is inconvenient to follow the letter of the law, but remember the Lord favors the righteous. People think, "I can go play soccer on Sunday just this once," or "I can go play in the championship game just this one time because my team needs me." You might hear, "If there is a special concert or event that only comes once in a lifetime, it is okay to attend on the Sabbath." Beware of these thoughts from the natural man since they teach principles contrary to the law of God. Think about what you are teaching those around you if every time there is a difficult or inconvenient decision, you decide not to follow the Lord. In life, our behaviors model our values and beliefs, and we need to be careful that we don't demonstrate that obedience is only necessary when it is easy. The Lord and the prophets have never taught the principle of inconvenient disobedience. Inconvenient disobedience means when things are hard it is okay not to follow the commandments of God.

Here is the principle of inconvenience that I want you to understand. *The greater the degree of difficulty in obedience, the greater the blessings offered.* Put another way, the greater the sacrifice, the greater the blessing. It is when things get tough that the Lord wants to know that we love Him. Anyone can love the Lord when they are sunbathing on the beach, sipping smoothies, and enjoying all of His creations. Those that really love the Lord are able to make hard decisions and do hard things. They are able to make decisions of faith that are not easy but that are absolutely righteous and rewarding. They are rewarding because they are rich in blessings. The thinking of the world—the natural man—does not sway these faithful followers of Christ; they are only swayed by truth, the word, and the Spirit of God.

In July of 2013, golfer Hunter Mahan had just finished the second round of the Canadian Open. He was leading the tournament by two strokes over the nearest competitor. He was playing well and was in control of a tournament that would pay the winner one million dollars. Just before the start of the third round on Saturday morning he received a phone call that his wife was going into labor. What a tough situation. What would you do? Hunter quickly withdrew from the golf tournament and flew home to be with his wife. Very early the next morning she gave birth to their first child Zoe.[2] Was it convenient? No. Was it the right decision? Absolutely. Hunter had decided that for him, it was family first. As missionaries, I invite you to make the decision to put obedience to God first, even when it is extremely inconvenient.

The missionaries that work the hardest, love the people the most, and exercise the most faith have the richest mission experiences. Why? They have made the most difficult of sacrifices. They have given their time, their talents, their energy, their mental capacities, and their hearts to the Lord. There is no thought of ignoring principles, handbook rules, mission guidelines, mission music choices, member visit rules, or any of the Lord's commandments. Their hearts have "no more disposition to do evil" (Mosiah 5:2). When they have a companion that makes obedience inconvenient, they stand up for what is right and

Critical Missionary Advice

continue to be faithful, despite the opposition. Inconvenience is never the easiest path but always has the most rewarding destination.

Remember Moroni's great counsel that you "receive no witness until after the trial of your faith" (Ether 12:6). Difficult decisions truly are trials of our faith, but the witness after the trial is worth every bit of inconvenience. I pray that when commandments are the hardest and most inconvenient, you will stand as a witness and obey the letter of the law. I pray that you will show the Lord you love Him through obedience, even in the most trying of times.

Your friend,
Brother Jeff Erickson

Critical Missionary
Advice

NOTES

1. "Rugby club to forfeit if scheduled to play Sunday," *KSL.com*, April 16, 2010, www.ksl.com/?sid=10419335.
2. Stephen Smith, "Hunter Mahan leaves $1 million PGA tournament he was winning to attend birth of child," *CBSNews.com*, July 29, 2013, www.cbsnews .com/news/hunter-mahan-leaves-1-million-pga-tournament-he-was-winning -to-attend-birth-of-child/.

A LITTLE PRIDE

Dear Elders and Sisters,

The book of Helaman shares a great phrase in the following verse, "And now it came to pass in the forty and third year of the reign of the judges, there was no contention among the people of Nephi save it were *a little pride* which was in the church, which did cause some little dissensions among the people, which affairs were settled in the ending of the forty and third year" (Helaman 3:1; emphasis added). The phrase "a little pride" carries great depth in this scripture. I have found that a little pride can be the start of something toxic in the life of a missionary.

When I had been in the mission field for about four months, I had the opportunity to train a new companion. By this time in my mission, I was overly confident in my abilities as a missionary and as a teacher. "A little pride" had crept into my heart, and I thought I was a much greater instrument than I truly was. I believed I was the best missionary—despite my many imperfections and weaknesses—and I certainly lacked the humility required of a humble servant of Christ. I had forgotten that the Lord is the teacher when it comes to the gospel of Jesus Christ.

As I trained my new companion, I was not very tolerant, patient, kind, or charitable. I was neither aware of my companion's struggles nor concerned with my critical responsibility of training him to be a powerful missionary. I thought if he just watched me he would become as great as I was. We were having success, but we weren't working together or having the kind of success we could have had working as one. This selfishness went on for two to three weeks until we had a zone conference and interviews with the mission president.

When I proudly walked in for my interview, I was prepared for praise. I felt we were doing great things in our area of service; we were teaching many people who were progressing and making commitments. I was filled with a little pride as I looked forward to my interview. I sat down, and my mission president proceeded to instruct, refine, and shape me in one of the most memorable interviews of my life. This good and deeply inspired president told me to get myself out of the limelight, quit focusing on elevating myself, and focus on the needs of my companion. He carefully and candidly taught me what it means to love someone more than you love yourself. He taught me that a missionary's true success is not found in individual success, but in success as a companionship. The Spirit was present, and I learned some valuable and life-changing principles that day. I am grateful my mission president had the wisdom to teach a young missionary how to be more humble and Christlike.

I have discovered that a little pride can carry a heavy price if we are not careful. As missionaries, a little pride can lead to a loss of the Spirit, a lack of humility, and an inability to heed the whisperings of the Spirit. Certainly, a little pride will not bless your life as you strive to become an instrument in the hands of God. As a bishop, I observed the harmful effects of pride; I witnessed it destroy marriages, ruin families, damage sacred parental relationships with children, and turn friends into enemies. I have seen pride produce immeasurable pain and suffering and cause many to be led away from righteousness and into sin and iniquity. Even a little pride truly causes a plethora of heartache and sorrow. A little pride will always be a big sin! President Uchtdorf said, "Pride is the great sin of self-elevation. . . . Pride is a deadly cancer."[1]

Alma's great question should be asked of every missionary: "Behold, are ye stripped of pride? I say unto you, if ye are not ye are not prepared to meet God" (Alma 5:28). Every elder or sister would do well to prepare to meet God by praying to eliminate pride. Jacob pled, "Let not this pride of your hearts destroy your souls!" (Jacob 2:16). Pride is never constructive, rather, it is always destructive.

One of the greatest warnings regarding pride was to Oliver Cowdery, a dear friend to the Prophet Joseph Smith. Oliver sat with Joseph during some of the most sacred times of our dispensation. It was Oliver who received the priesthood from the hands of John the

Baptist. It was Oliver who was the first to be baptized by Joseph during the period of the Restoration. It was Oliver who was chosen as scribe for the Book of Mormon. It was Oliver who was selected as one of the Three Witnesses of the Book of Mormon. It was Oliver who played an important role in the Restoration of the gospel of Jesus Christ. It was Oliver whom Joseph leaned on in many instances as the Restoration unfolded.

The Lord said to Oliver, "Behold, I speak unto you, Oliver, a few words. Behold, thou art blessed, and art under no condemnation. But beware of pride, lest thou shouldst enter into temptation" (D&C 23:1). Oliver didn't heed that very personal warning, and his pride led him away from the Church and away from choice blessings for many years. For Oliver, pride truly was "a snare upon [his] soul" (D&C 90:17). As missionaries, may we be wiser than Oliver Cowdery and heed the warning to "beware of pride."

Pride never invites the Spirit of God, and successful missionaries must have the Spirit or they cannot teach. The Lord said that when we "gratify our pride . . . the Spirit of the Lord is grieved" (D&C 121:37). President Benson taught, "Pride does not look up to God and care about what is right. It looks sideways to man and argues who is right. Pride is manifest in the spirit of contention."[2] May we eliminate our pride so the Spirit may be more abundant in our lives and in our teachings. May we remember that a little pride is a sin and only the beginning of more pride.

My son Taft taught me some important lessons in a simple experience we had. A few years ago, I came home from work and wanted to spend some time with my sons playing in the backyard. I said to three of my boys, "Who wants to kick the soccer ball with me?" Two of my sons quickly said, "I do, I do." My four-year-old, Taft, said, "I don't." I was surprised since he was usually the first to want to spend time kicking the soccer ball. I looked at him and said, "Huh?" He proudly said, "I am already good, Dad." I learned a few lessons from young Taft. First, confidence is wonderful, as it is important to feel good about yourself. Second, may we never be so confident that we don't continue to humbly learn, progress, and be taught by a wise Heavenly Father. Third, may we never forget that God can teach us anything if we are humble, no matter how good we already are.

President Benson reminded us, "The antidote for pride is humility—meekness, submissiveness. . . . It is the broken heart and contrite spirit. . . . Let us choose to be humble. We can do it. I know we can."[3] May your confidence in the Lord continue to blossom through humbly trusting Him.

Your friend,
Brother Jeff Erickson

NOTES

1.   Dieter F. Uchtdorf, "Pride and the Priesthood," *Ensign*, November 2010.
2.   Ezra Taft Benson, "Cleansing the Inner Vessel," *Ensign*, May 1986.
3.   Ezra Taft Benson, "Beware of Pride," *Ensign*, May 1989.

KNOW THE MASTER

Dear Elders and Sisters,

A few years ago, our family traveled to Utah and stayed at the home of some relatives. We were carrying our luggage into their house when we rounded a corner and my four-year-old son Blake saw a picture of the Savior on their wall. He looked at the painting and inquisitively said, "Hey, they know Jesus?"

There are many things you will learn on your mission. There are many principles, truths, doctrines, and covenants that you will understand and appreciate more than you ever have. There is *one* thing you must know before you come home that is more important than anything else: you must come to know the Master.

King Benjamin said, "For how knoweth a man the master whom he has not served, and who is a stranger unto him, and is far from the thoughts and intents of his heart?" (Mosiah 5:13). Think of the experiences you have had when you felt close to the Master. When the thoughts you had and your deepest desires and intentions were focused on Christ and His work. Those are the times when you come to know Him better because you see His hand, His work, His miracles, and His divine tender mercies. The missionaries who serve Him best come to know Him the best.

As a missionary, I had my "wall of fame" above my missionary desk at each apartment I lived in. I had a picture of myself and two buddies, a few small motivational quotes, a picture of Brooke Shields (given to me by the daughter of a lady we taught), and a picture of Christ. I may have had a few other things, but I can't remember anymore. I probably didn't need the picture of Brooke Shields (it was a very modest picture, by the way), but it did serve as a conversation piece. The Brooke Shields

Coming to the Savior

59

picture was signed in black marker, "Brooke Shields." It was a little 5 × 7 poster that came with the Brooke Shields doll when you bought it. On the poster, I added in black marker, "To Jeff, With Love." It then looked like a personally written note saying, "To Jeff, With Love, Brooke Shields." When visiting elders would come into my apartment, they would look at this wall and almost all of them would ask, "Do you know her?" I would say "yes," tell a little story, and have a little fun, but in the end, I would reveal that I didn't know her at all; I had just been a fan of hers prior to my mission, and the poster was a reminder of the little girl we taught.

Right next to the Brooks Shields picture on my wall was my picture of Christ. Never during my entire mission, did I have a missionary come in and ask, "Do you know Him?" I probably wouldn't have asked that either, but in thinking of the experience, I learned a very valuable lesson. If the question were asked, what would my answer be? I believe my answer would have been deeply heartfelt and true. Throughout my mission, I really did come to know Christ, and I continue to feel that I know Him in a very personal way. I don't know everything about Him, but I am still continuing to learn of Him as I serve Him. I feel that He is close to my thoughts, and, hopefully, my actions are directed by His teachings and my faith in Him. I testify that He is the Son of God and the light and the way.

I have seen missionaries come home after their missions and speak of Christ with love and tenderness and great depth. I could tell they had come to know Him in a more profound way because I could feel it. I have seen others who have been very careless in their mission service that speak of the Savior casually, and I could feel the distance between them and Christ. Make sure that if you learn anything as a missionary, you learn to know Christ, and come home knowing that Christ is the centerpiece of everything in your life. "And this is life eternal, that they might know thee the only true God, and Jesus Christ, whom thou hast sent" (John 17:3).

When my son Tyler was three years old, he was a vivid dreamer and a light sleeper, which made for some great late night experiences. One night at about 3:00 a.m., he screamed, "Dad, Dad!" I went to his bed and said, "Tyler, what is it?" To which he responded, "Dad, I'm all alone in here." For this little three-year-old, it was a scary feeling to be

Coming to the Savior

all alone. In reflecting on this experience, I was powerfully reminded that we are never really alone. There is always a loving Heavenly Father near us who watches over us and will always hear us. We can call out, "Father, Father," and he will come and comfort us and help us not to feel alone. I believe this is one of the most important reasons to come to know God and Jesus Christ. You must come to know that when you are lonely, in despair, or in need of heavenly assistance, you can call out, "Father, help me in my loneliness or my trial" and he will be there to answer your prayer. Through the Atonement of Jesus Christ, you will find strength, compassion, comfort, peace, and an always-attentive Father.

As a missionary, as you serve our Heavenly Father and our Savior Jesus Christ faithfully, you will come to know Them deeply. Much of the world has forgotten Them, and it has brought great despair, loneliness, tragedy, wickedness, selfishness, and misdirection. God needs a people full of love and a faith in Christ. True faith will only come through knowing Him. I pray that you will come to know Heavenly Father and His Son, Jesus Christ, more completely than you have ever known Them before.

Your friend,
Brother Jeff Erickson

Coming to
the Savior

WAITING ON THE LORD

Dear Elders and Sisters,

One week in Sunday school, we studied the principle of waiting on the Lord. I have come to learn that waiting on the Lord brings richer results than we could ever imagine. The Psalmist said, "I waited patiently for the Lord; and he inclined unto me, and heard my cry" (Psalm 40:1).

The "Stanford marshmallow experiment" was a series of studies on delayed gratification in the late 1960s and early 1970s. In these experiments, children were given a treat and two choices. They could immediately eat the treat, or they could wait fifteen minutes and receive an additional treat. The tester would put a marshmallow, pretzel, or cookie in front of the child, leave the room, and the child would be left to make the decision. After fifteen minutes, the tester would return to see if the children had eaten the treat or if they had waited for a better reward. For children ages four to six, this was a difficult test. One-third of the six hundred children who were originally studied were able to delay gratification and receive the greater reward: a second marshmallow.

Follow-up studies done on these test groups have provided a few fascinating conclusions. One conclusion of the tests showed that those able to patiently wait for rewards by delaying gratification tended to have better life outcomes as measured by other variables.[1]

I believe the same principle is absolutely true spiritually. When we wait on the Lord and trust in Him, life's outcomes are better. God knows what we need, and if we can righteously wait, He will reward us accordingly with abundant blessings. The key ingredient to waiting is to do so in righteousness.

Zacharias and Elizabeth waited on the Lord for decades to have a son. They had prayed for days, weeks, months, and eventually years and decades to finally receive the answer to their tireless prayer. When the answer came, Zacharias could hardly believe it since he had prayed so long. When the angel came to Zacharias, he said, "thy prayer is heard" (Luke 1:13). After so many years of seemingly unanswered prayers, Zacharias struggled with the revelation from the angel and was punished for his unbelief for a time. The angel said, "And, behold, thou shalt be dumb, and not able to speak, until the day that these things shall be performed, because thou believest not my words, which shall be fulfilled in their season" (Luke 1:20). Zacharias may have forgotten in a small way what he was truly waiting for. The angel taught this good man a few critical principles about waiting on the Lord before he left him. He told him how much joy this son would bring and how wonderful he would be.

> [He will] be great in the sight of the Lord . . . and he shall be filled with the Holy Ghost. . . .
>
> And many of the children of Israel shall he turn to the Lord their God. . . .
>
> And the disobedient to the wisdom of the just; . . . [and that he would] make ready a people prepared for the Lord. (Luke 1:15–17)

Why did the angel share these precious insights into the life of John the Baptist? I don't know all of the reasons, but I know one of them. A patient and faithful mother had also been praying for decades, and she and her husband wanted to know why the Lord waited so long to grant a righteous desire. Understanding was given to them in the treasured insights about John. They had waited on the Lord for a long time because the precious blessing would be so great. One of the treasured blessings was that John would be "great in the sight of the Lord" (Luke 1:15).

The Lord has promised, "Waiting patiently on the Lord, for your prayers have entered into the ears of the Lord of Sabaoth, and are recorded with this seal and testament—the Lord hath sworn and decreed that they shall be granted" (D&C 98:2). The Lord promises that righteous desires will be granted to the righteous. We must be patient, and pray that our desires might be righteous and in accordance with the will of God. We only need to look to faithful saints like Elisabeth and Zacharias to know that these promises are true.

There are two critical principles with corresponding promises that come when we faithfully wait on the Lord. When we wait on the Lord, we will eventually see the "whys." Why did the Lord make us wait so long? Why didn't He answer my prayer before? Why didn't He answer my prayer in the way I wanted? Why didn't He bless me with what appeared to be a righteous desire? For the righteous, every "why" will be answered in due time. "And he that will not harden his heart, to him is given the greater portion of the word, until it is given unto him to know the mysteries of God until he know them in full" (Alma 12:10).

The second principle is the answer to a soul-searching question: will it be worth the wait? The answer is a resounding "yes." The Lord's promises are sure. The Lord's blessings are abundant. The Lord's plan is powerful. The Lord's ways are higher than the ways of man. The richness of the blessing will far surpass the trial of waiting. Whether in this life or the next, we will see the wisdom of God and know and understand that the blessing was well worth the wait.

In reflecting on this lesson, I thought of a few amazing families in our ward who have children with some physical and mental challenges. These stripling spirits were sent to earth to take upon themselves compromised physical bodies with a variety of impairments or diseases. Their valiant parents then do all they can as they wait on the Lord. They look forward to one day knowing these celestial spirits will be free of impairment. I know a loving Heavenly Father gives them doctrines, experiences, insights, and treasured moments that help along the way. The greatest blessing and most sacred moment will truly come after waiting when they come to know these children in their perfected forms. When these faithful parents see them as they really are they will say, "Father, I see and I understand, I now know why you made us wait." They will marvel at the power, valiance, strength, and depth of these stripling souls.

Missionaries must often wait on the Lord for a variety of blessings, such as a change of heart in their investigators, fulfilled commitments, increased strength in their own testimonies, help with companions, and miracles. As a missionary, you will recognize the power of this verse as you wait on the Lord: "But they that wait upon the Lord shall renew their strength; they shall mount up with wings as eagles; they shall run, and not be weary; and they shall walk, and not faint" (Isaiah 40:31).

Your friend,
Brother Jeff Erickson

Coming to
the Savior

NOTES

1. Jonah Lehrer, "Don't! The secret of self-control," *The New Yorker*, May 18, 2009.

YOUR FOUNDATION

Dear Elders and Sisters,

As a missionary, you are called to preach faith in Jesus Christ, repentance, baptism, the Holy Ghost, and enduring to the end. I love all of these messages. At the center of this message, I hope you always remember to powerfully convey that Christ is the sure foundation, whereon if we build we will never fall. Remember these words:

> And now, my sons, remember, remember that it is upon the rock of our Redeemer, who is Christ, the Son of God, that ye must build your foundation; that when the devil shall send forth his mighty winds, yea, his shafts in the whirlwind, yea, when all his hail and his mighty storm shall beat upon you, it shall have no power over you to drag you down to the gulf of misery and endless wo, because of the rock upon which ye are built, which is a sure foundation, a foundation whereon if men build they cannot fall. (Helaman 5:12)

We are told that the foundation of the Salt Lake Temple in some places is thirty-two feet deep.[1] "Deep excavations around the Salt Lake Temple in 1963 revealed a 14-foot-deep granite foundation, atop a 16-foot-deep sandstone foundation."[2] Why would the early Saints fortify the temple with such depth and use such strong materials? The granite was incredibly heavy and hard to retrieve as the stone was at a quarry twenty miles away from the temple site. President Young said, "When the Temple is built I want it to stand through the millennium, in connection with many others that will yet be built."[3] The Lord wants that wonderful temple to stand forever. How could it stand forever with a weak and unfortified foundation? It couldn't! How can we stand eternally if we do not have a deep and fortified foundation? The gospel of Jesus Christ has the surest of all foundations: Jesus Christ Himself. The gospel and the Church will never fall, no matter how

Coming to the Savior

great the storm of the world, because their foundation is the strongest foundation there is.

Author Jerry Earl Johnson tells of a time when he was speaking in a prison to a group of female prisoners. He says, "I asked how many of them had been betrayed by a man. Every hand went up. Then I pointed to the solitary painting of Christ on the wall. 'He will never do that to you,' I said."[4] Jesus Christ will never betray us as our sure foundation; we can put our trust in Him.

May these words be the foundation of your invitation to those you teach: "And now, my beloved brethren, I would that ye should come unto Christ, who is the Holy One of Israel, and partake of his salvation, and the power of his redemption. Yea, come unto him, and offer your whole souls as an offering unto him, and continue in fasting and praying, and endure to the end; and as the Lord liveth ye will be saved" (Omni 1:26). May we always be like the wise man the Savior spoke of in Matthew.

> Therefore whosoever heareth these sayings of mine, and doeth them, I will liken him unto a wise man, which built his house upon a rock:
>
> And the rain descended, and the floods came, and the winds blew, and beat upon that house; and it fell not: for it was founded upon a rock. (Matthew 7:24–25)

As you teach, may you echo Nephi, who said, "And we talk of Christ, we rejoice in Christ, we preach of Christ, we prophesy of Christ, and we write according to our prophecies, that our children may know to what source they may look for a remission of their sins" (2 Nephi 25:26). May you help the people of your mission understand this critical truth: "And now, my son, I have told you this that ye may learn wisdom, that ye may learn of me that there is no other way or means whereby man can be saved, only in and through Christ. Behold, he is the life and the light of the world. Behold, he is the word of truth and righteousness" (Alma 38:9). May you know and testify of these principles:

> And thus he shall bring salvation to all those who shall believe on his name; this being the intent of this last sacrifice, to bring about the bowels of mercy, which overpowereth justice, and bringeth about means unto men that they may have faith unto repentance.

And thus mercy can satisfy the demands of justice, and encircles them in the arms of safety, while he that exercises no faith unto repentance is exposed to the whole law of the demands of justice; therefore only unto him that has faith unto repentance is brought about the great and eternal plan of redemption. (Alma 34:15–16)

President Thomas S. Monson shared this great story:

At the time I met him, President Tanner was president of the vast Trans-Canada Pipelines, Ltd., and president of the Canada Calgary Stake. He was known as "Mr. Integrity" in Canada. During that first meeting, we discussed, among other subjects, the cold Canadian winters, where storms rage, temperatures can linger well below freezing for weeks at a time, and where icy winds lower those temperatures even further. I asked President Tanner why the roads and highways in western Canada basically remained intact during such winters, showing little or no signs of cracking or breaking, while the road surfaces in many areas where winters are less cold and less severe developed cracks and breaks and potholes.

Said he, "The answer is in the depth of the base of the paving materials. In order for them to remain strong and unbroken, it is necessary to go very deep with the foundation layers. When the foundations are not deep enough, the surfaces cannot withstand the extremes of weather."

Over the years I have thought often of this conversation and of President Tanner's explanation, for I recognize in his words a profound application for our lives. Stated simply, if we do not have a deep foundation of faith and a solid testimony of truth, we may have difficulty withstanding the harsh storms and icy winds of adversity which inevitably come to each of us.[5]

I am grateful to have a personal testimony of Christ. May we never forget, amidst the tumult of the battle for truth, that He is the Creator of the earth, the Messiah, the Prince of Peace, the Holy One, the centerpiece of the plan, and "the way, the truth, and the life" (John 14:6). Jesus Christ is the only reason for hope, and the only one that can and will change our lives forever. The birth and mission of Jesus Christ is the most important event in history. "O remember, remember, my sons, the words which king Benjamin spake unto his people; yea, remember that there is no other way nor means whereby man can be saved, only through the atoning blood of Jesus Christ, who shall come;

Coming to
the Savior

yea, remember that he cometh to redeem the world" (Helaman 5:9). I testify that he truly is the "foundation whereon if men build they cannot fall" (Helaman 5:12).

Your friend,
Brother Jeff Erickson

NOTES

1. Boyd K. Packer, "A Temple to Exalt," *Ensign*, August 1993.
2. Lynn Arave, "Symbolism can be seen in architecture of S. L. Temple," *Deseret News*, November 27, 2008.
3. Packer, "A Temple to Exalt."
4. Jerry Earl Johnston, *Rescued: A Prodigal's Journey Home* (American Fork, Utah: Covenant, 2012), 103.
5. Thomas S. Monson, "How Firm a Foundation," *Ensign*, November 2006.

Coming to
the Savior

TEACHER

Dear Elders and Sisters,

I had an experience with my daughter Holland that reminded me why correct and good teaching is so critical in all that we do. Holland was helping me install light bulbs in the house, and she excitedly retrieved a small two-foot ladder as I retrieved my eight-foot ladder. We found a light bulb that didn't work in the bathroom, and I told Holland to set up her ladder, climb the ladder to the counter, and then climb on the counter, and I would be right back with a light bulb. When I returned to the bathroom with the light bulb, she was crying. When the tears stopped, she showed me what had happened. She had propped up the ladder without unfolding it, and as she tried to climb up, it collapsed to the ground and so did she. Fortunately, she was not badly hurt. I realized she had never before used a folding ladder by herself. I then taught her how to unfold the little ladder and make sure the extra arms were straight. She observed this teaching, and she unfolded and set up her ladder as instructed, and successfully replaced the bathroom light bulb with my help. After performing this task four different times, she was thrilled by her efforts in changing light bulbs. The ladder experience with Holland reminded me again that we are always teachers.

I want to discuss the role and the goals of a teacher. What is a teacher, who can be a teacher, and how does a real teacher teach? I have to start with the master teacher and one of the ultimate compliments paid to Him: "The same came to Jesus by night, and said unto him, Rabbi, we know that thou art a teacher come from God: for no man can do these miracles that thou doest, except God be with him" (John 3:2). How do we become "a teacher come from God" like Christ?

One of the great blessings of being a missionary is being set apart as a teacher. The Lord gives all of His servants the power to teach.

> Wherefore, I the Lord ask you this question—unto what were ye ordained?
>
> To preach my gospel by the Spirit, even the Comforter which was sent forth to teach the truth (D&C 50:13–14).

The Lord ordains and sets apart His servants, and then it is up to them to become proficient at teaching by the Spirit. Truly, this is a gift that is earned and not just granted:

> Verily I say unto you, he that is ordained of me and sent forth to preach the word of truth by the Comforter, in the Spirit of truth, doth he preach it by the Spirit of truth or some other way?
>
> And if it be by some other way it is not of God. (D&C 50:17–18)

How do you obtain the Spirit and how do you teach with the Spirit? You do what both the ancient and modern prophets have done. You follow the example of the best missionaries. A great model is found in the missions of Ammon and Aaron.

> Now these sons of Mosiah were with Alma at the time the angel first appeared unto him; therefore Alma did rejoice exceedingly to see his brethren; and what added more to his joy, they were still his brethren in the Lord; yea, and they had waxed strong in the knowledge of the truth; for they were men of a sound understanding and they had searched the scriptures diligently, that they might know the word of God.
>
> But this is not all; they had given themselves to much prayer, and fasting; therefore they had the spirit of prophecy, and the spirit of revelation, and when they taught, they taught with power and authority of God. (Alma 17:2–3)

There is a price to pay to be a master teacher. The price is personal righteousness. The price is prayer, study, desire, fasting, diligence, and obedience. The price is the love of the people you teach. The price is believing that you are no greater a teacher than the receiver of the message like we read in Alma: "And the priest, not esteeming himself above his hearers, for the preacher was no better than the hearer, neither was the teacher any better than the learner; and thus they were all equal, and they did all labor, every man according to his strength" (Alma 1:26). Many missionaries feel they are greater than the people of their mission, which is never the case in Heavenly Father's plan. We are all children of a loving God, who wants everyone to come back home. Here is a promise I love for those earnest teachers who seek the Spirit, "And the Spirit shall be given unto you by the prayer of faith; and if ye receive not the Spirit ye shall not teach" (D&C 42:14).

Early in the history of the Church, Oliver Cowdery and Sidney Rigdon were both powerful teachers. Here is the experience of a young lawyer as he listened to Oliver and Sidney teach the gospel:

> Apparently at a later Sunday, after Rigdon's baptism and ordination, Varnum J. Card came to Mayfield accompanied by his friend John Barr. Cowdery and Rigdon spoke at a morning meeting, and Rigdon baptized in mid-afternoon. In the midst of a moving service, "Mr. Card suddenly seized my arm and said, 'Take me away.'" Card's face was "pale," and "his frame trembled as we walked away and mounted our horses." Regaining his composure, Varnum Card evaluated his experience: "Mr. Barr, if you had not been there, I certainly should have gone into the water." He said the impulse was irresistible.[1]

Here are two virtues of an effective teacher of the gospel of Jesus Christ. One is this: "And also trust no one to be your teacher nor your minister, except he be a man of God, walking in his ways and keeping his commandments" (Mosiah 23:14). Obviously, with teaching comes great responsibility and personal obedience. The second virtue is: "Wherefore, he that preacheth and he that receiveth, understand one another, and both are edified and rejoice together" (D&C 50:22). The beauty of being a minister of the gospel of Christ is when you teach with the Spirit, the people are edified. When they are edified, they feel and act on the Spirit, and you rejoice together. True rejoicing brings change, peace, desire, and a newfound love of eternal truths. True rejoicing is what really makes a mission so wonderful. When people are baptized and reactivated due to spiritual promptings, there is reason to rejoice.

My favorite elementary school teacher was Mrs. Greer; I loved her. She had an impact on me as a third grader, because she loved me. Nearly forty years later, I found myself praying in the temple one day over a troubling business matter. Sister Greer, my old third-grade teacher was working in the temple that day, and I visited with her for a few minutes. During those precious moments, she asked me a few questions. One of the questions she asked me was an inspired question about the matter over which I was praying. There is no way on earth she could have ever known. Her faith-filled and inspired response was "Oh, don't you worry about it, it will all work out." She had no idea that I needed to hear those words; she was certainly an answer to my prayer that day as I sought the Lord's guidance. A loving Heavenly Father had lifted my burden, answered my prayer, and comforted my soul through a wise teacher whom I greatly loved and respected. We need to have missionaries who are inspired teachers, who know what to say, and who know what questions to ask as Sister Greer did on that sacred occasion.

A great scriptural example of a teacher and a receiver being edified and rejoicing together is found in the exchange between Aaron and King Lamoni's father. The Lord had prepared the king to receive Aaron's message. Aaron had built a relationship of trust, and then built on that trust as he began to teach the king simple truths. Aaron knew the Spirit was edifying the King when he heard these precious words, "And if now thou sayest there is a God, behold I will believe" (Alma 22:7). The next verse tells us, "And now when Aaron heard this, his heart began to rejoice, and he said: Behold, assuredly as thou livest, O king, there is a God" (Alma 22:8). The edifying and rejoicing only continued as the King said, "Yea, I believe that the Great Spirit created all things, and I desire that ye should tell me concerning all these things, and I will believe thy words" (Alma 22:11). I can feel the spirit of rejoicing when I read the king's heartfelt prayer. He says, "Oh God . . . I will give away all my sins to know thee" (Alma 22:18).

I pray that as you teach by the Spirit, like Aaron did, you will have an abundance of edifying and rejoicing with those people you teach.

Your friend,
Brother Jeff Erickson

NOTES

1. Richard Lloyd Anderson, "The Impact of the First Preaching in Ohio," *BYU Studies*, vol. 11, no. 3 (1971).

THE AMMON MODEL

Dear Elders and Sisters,

I want to discuss what I call "the Ammon Model." Let's take a look at what Ammon did as a missionary, as well as the attributes he had that made him so successful as an emissary of Jesus Christ.

He had the desire to be a missionary. "Yea, I desire to dwell among this people for a time" (Alma 17:23). Ammon really wanted to be where he was. Maybe it wasn't the best mission in the world, but he *wanted* to be where he was called, and he was going to stay there until his work was done. He desired to be on a mission, he desired to save souls, and he desired to serve the people of Lamoni. Although for you this is just a two-year or eighteen-month visit, let the people know that if you could, you would stay there forever.

He served the people. The King was impressed with Ammon and offered him one of his daughters, and Ammon essentially said, "No, thank you. I don't date or pursue relationships as a missionary." Ammon went on to say, "Nay, but I will be thy servant. Therefore Ammon became a servant to king Lamoni" (Alma 17:25). Like Ammon, you should absolutely serve the people of your mission. A true servant will serve at any opportunity, pray for the people, build them up, love them completely, and share with them the things that will bless their lives the most. Like the Savior said, "For he that is least among you all, the same shall be great" (Luke 9:48).

He looked for inspired opportunities. Remember Ammon's feelings once the flocks were scattered? "Now when Ammon saw this his heart was swollen within him with joy; for, said he, I will show forth my power unto these my fellow-servants, or the power which is in me, in restoring these flocks unto the king, that I may win the hearts of

Becoming a
Better Teacher

these my fellow-servants, that I may lead them to believe in my words" (Alma 17:29). Ammon wasn't trying to make himself look good, he was just trying to find inspired ways to touch the hearts of the people. He recognized when the Lord opened a window of opportunity, and he fearlessly moved forward. Look for inspired opportunities to impact those you teach and those you minister.

He was a true friend. Listen to the summary of what the Lamanites felt after watching Ammon fight the men at the waters of Sebus: "Therefore, we know that he is a friend to the king" (Alma 18:3). Be willing to do anything for the people you teach, in righteousness, of course. Be a true friend to them. Love them, share with them, and invite them with the Spirit. Ask them to change; only a true friend will invite someone to do the right things.

He astonished those around him with his faithfulness. "Now when king Lamoni heard that Ammon was preparing his horses and his chariots he was more astonished, because of the faithfulness of Ammon, saying: Surely there has not been any servant among all my servants that has been so faithful as this man; for even he doth remember all my commandments to execute them" (Alma 18:10). Let the people of your mission know of your goodness and faithfulness. Let them know that you love the Lord and His principles, and that they make you who you are. Too many missionaries are not obeying rules, not being faithful, and are doing things of the world. Maybe they are getting up late, wasting precious time, looking "faddish" as a missionary, or trying to be cool rather than righteous. Let the people of your mission know that, above all else, you are faithful to God and the principles of the gospel of Jesus Christ. The people of your mission don't need cool, they need faithful.

He took the right approach to the people of his area. "I say unto you, what is it, that thy marvelings are so great? Behold, I am a man, and am thy servant; therefore, whatsoever thou desirest which is right, that will I do" (Alma 18:17). This is what your investigators should know of you. You are their servant, and whatever is right, you will do for them.

What was the result of the "Ammon Model"? "Now Ammon being wise, yet harmless, he said unto Lamoni: Wilt thou hearken unto my words, if I tell thee by what power I do these things? And this is the thing that I desire of thee" (Alma 18:22). When Lamoni and the

Lamanites knew who Ammon really was (an obedient representative of Christ in word and deed), they would believe everything and anything that he said. The teaching moment came after they witnessed the integrity, honor, and character of Ammon.

It is my prayer that as you follow the Ammon Model, you will have experiences like he had—not experiences where you are slaying others, but experiences where you have the trust of the people you love and teach. When the honest in heart know you, they will be willing to listen to your message. Like Ammon's experience with Lamoni, the Lord and the Spirit will then perform the miracle of conversion.

Your friend,
Brother Jeff Erickson

Becoming a
Better Teacher

TRAINER

Dear Elders and Sisters,

Many years ago, I went on a three-day rafting trip on the Rogue River in Oregon. I went with a group of dental students as well as a professor who had been a professional guide on the river, having traveled the river many times. Most of us had never really rafted before, but we all completely trusted our guide. He taught us how to paddle and how to turn and maneuver effectively. He taught us to be safe on the river as it could turn deadly in seconds. During his instruction, the water was calm, and I felt that his warning was overkill and more than we needed. However, in the most difficult and treacherous parts of the river, I quickly learned how wonderful it was to have a wise and experienced guide as my instructor.

There were many dangerous spots in the river where boats had flipped, then been trapped, and people had drowned. As we negotiated these areas, we did exactly as our guide instructed, and made it through safely. There were times when our instructions were "Just follow me, and do as I do." When we followed precisely, we were safely directed through treacherous rapids. At times, we watched other boaters struggle in different areas of the river, but by following our guide, our struggles were minimized. Rafting on the Rogue River was a memorable, safe, and wonderful trip because we had a wise and trusted guide.

I want to discuss what the ideal missionary trainer should be. What is a trainer? A trainer is a coach, teacher, guide, instructor, mentor, tutor, and leader. What do trainers do? They direct, lead, show the way, advise, influence, pilot, or steer. I think the most powerful word of those used to describe a trainer is "guide." The word *guide* truly reminds me of the word *shepherd*. A trainer must be a spiritual shepherd.

The Savior was the master trainer. When you look to Him as a coach, teacher, and mentor, there has obviously been no better trainer than the Savior. How do you follow this example and become a master trainer? By following the words of the Good Shepherd. As a missionary trainer, you have been given a sacred responsibility to train a future powerful missionary. Don't treat this responsibility lightly. You are training a mother's son or daughter whose family is praying for his or her success. Good parents are praying for their missionary to change into the young stripling warrior they have always hoped for them to be. In many instances, a missionary's first two to three months of their mission is a reflection of the rest of their mission. Here are some attributes you need as you approach this sacred trust of training: "And no one can assist in this work except he shall be humble and full of love, having faith, hope, and charity, being temperate in all things, whatsoever shall be entrusted to his care" (D&C 12:8). I love that Heavenly Father trusts trainers with the future of His next great emissaries.

Here are some words given to Oliver Cowdery that helped him as a leader in the early Church. These words are a blessing to one who trains a missionary companion: "Admonish him in his faults, and also receive admonition of him. Be patient; be sober; be temperate; have patience, faith, hope and charity" (D&C 6:19). You won't be perfect as a trainer, so please don't expect perfection from the missionary you are training either. Remember, the best teachers always continue to learn from their students.

One of the great trainers in the Book of Mormon was Alma. When Amulek (the junior companion) met Alma, he said, "I know that thou wilt be a blessing unto me and my house" (Alma 8:20). Alma had taken a "green" companion in Amulek and he "administered unto him in his tribulations, and strengthened him in the Lord" (Alma 15:18). *Administer* means to look after, supervise, direct, or govern someone.[1] To *strengthen* someone means to fortify, reinforce, support, bolster, or boost.[2] What a blessing to have someone who would love you enough to do that for you.

Here is an idea of the pattern that Alma and Amulek's companionship followed.

And Alma tarried many days with Amulek before he began to preach unto the people. . . .

And the word came to Alma, saying: Go; and also say unto my servant Amulek, go forth and prophesy unto this people, saying— Repent ye, for thus saith the Lord, except ye repent I will visit this people in mine anger; yea, and I will not turn my fierce anger away.

And Alma went forth, and also Amulek, among the people, to declare the words of God unto them; and they were filled with the Holy Ghost.

And they had power given unto them. . . . Now, this was done that the Lord might show forth his power in them.

And it came to pass that they went forth and began to preach and to prophesy unto the people, according to the spirit and power which the Lord had given them. (Alma 8:27, 29–32)

Follow Alma's training of Amulek and teach your companion the word as well as what to preach. Help them understand the importance of inviting people to repent. Teach them to come unto Christ, be filled with the Holy Ghost, remember God will give them power, and finally, go and do.

To be effective with this missionary pattern, you need to have these trainer attributes:

And faith, hope, charity and love, with an eye single to the glory of God, qualify him for the work.

Remember faith, virtue, knowledge, temperance, patience, brotherly kindness, godliness, charity, humility, diligence. (D&C 4:5–6)

These attributes will help you to utilize the "powers of heaven" (D&C 121:36) in your work, your training, and your companionship.

Finally, the sons of Mosiah were sent off on incredibly successful missions by their "trainer"—Ammon. We read, "Now Ammon being the chief among them, or rather he did administer unto them, and he departed from them, after having blessed them according to their several stations, having imparted the word of God unto them, or administered unto them before his departure; and thus they took their several journeys throughout the land" (Alma 17:18). Ammon blessed them, taught them, and administered to them, and then they went to their areas of labor. I believe that is what a master trainer should do—bless, teach, and administer. May you do those things as you become a trainer and a shepherd.

A few years ago, I took a two-day rappelling course with a qualified trainer. The instruction, teaching, and guidance were excellent. I enjoyed the experience and the newfound knowledge that was being shared. A critical part of the training was the application of the knowledge. There was a point in the training where I had to descend from a one-hundred-foot cliff, trusting my trainer, the equipment, and what I had been taught. On the top of the cliff, the wind was blowing, the top was narrow, and I was afraid of the height. With the trainer's guidance, I descended successfully without incident, despite some fears and concerns that I had.

I believe young elders and sisters trust their mission trainers in a similar fashion. They are young, eager, and apprehensive while attempting to learn to be effective servants placing trust in the faith, knowledge, and tools that their trainers are sharing with them. May you shepherd them and help them to successfully and safely plant their feet on the ground without incident.

**Your friend,
Brother Jeff Erickson**

NOTES

1.   *Merriam-Webster Thesaurus*, s.v. "administer," accessed February 27, 2017, www.merriam-webster.com/thesaurus/administer.
2.   *Merriam-Webster Thesaurus,* s.v. "strengthen," accessed February 27, 2017, www.merriam-webster.com/thesaurus/strengthen.

"BE THOU AN EXAMPLE OF THE BELIEVERS"

Dear Elders and Sisters,

Having seven children, I've become pretty good at making school lunches over the years. Most days the sandwiches consist of ham, turkey, cheese, and a few other condiments. In all my sandwich-making years, I constantly struggle to get my kids to take a sandwich that contains the heel (the end piece) of the loaf of bread. No matter how much turkey or lettuce or how many pickles I put on a sandwich, if it has the heel, I still can't convince an eleven-year-old or a fifteen-year-old to put it in their lunch sack. For some reason, the end of the bread doesn't represent real bread to any of my children.

My kids will grab a brown bag and load their lunch, but before loading a sandwich, they will inspect both sides to see if it is "good bread" and not the heel. They don't usually take the time to examine what is on the inside, but they do evaluate the outside crust of the bread. I will frequently make seven or eight sandwiches and leave them on the counter and each of my six sons and my one daughter will take one or two and put them in their lunch. When all of my children are gone to school, one sandwich will remain, and it is always the one with the not-worthy-of-eating heel. In my home, when it comes to sandwiches, the outward appearance seems to count for everything.

For many people, as they evaluate the gospel of Jesus Christ, they will only see the outside at first—the crust or the heel. Missionaries, in many instances, are the only crust or exterior of the gospel of Jesus Christ that people will see. So, the question becomes, how do you make the gospel look to them? Do you truly reflect what is on the inside?

Paul said, "Let no man despise thy youth; but be thou an example of the believers, in word, in conversation, in charity, in spirit, in faith, in purity" (1 Timothy 4:12). Paul teaches us that in these six significant areas we need to be "saints." By becoming saints, we come to live what we teach, rather than be hypocrites. A saint's life reflects the truthfulness of the gospel to those who may evaluate the gospel solely based on a representative; a hypocrite's life does not. Job posed this thought-provoking question, "For what is the hope of the hypocrite, though he hath gained, when God taketh away his soul?" (Job 27:8). A missionary who believes and lives what he teaches is a powerful teacher. A missionary who insincerely testifies of principles he does not live is without power and without the Spirit. No man or woman who ever lives will "dupe" the Spirit or our Heavenly Father. Individuals may sometimes deceive bishops, stake presidents, friends, and family, but God will not be mocked.

Being an example of the believers in "word and conversation" as Paul says means that our speech is pure and undefiled. It means our speech elevates and inspires. It means that we never speak evil or ill of others. It means that our words are thoughtful, kind, wise, prudent, instructional, and most importantly, edifying. What would a stranger think of you just based on overhearing your speech? Would you inspire others to be better and come to know Christ? May our words and conversation be inspired of God as Mormon said, "But behold, that which is of God inviteth and enticeth to do good continually; wherefore, every thing which inviteth and enticeth to do good, and to love God, and to serve him, is inspired of God" (Moroni 7:13).

Elder Robert K. Dellenbach shared this story:

I know of a man named Tom who agreed to drive his son Michael and some of Michael's soccer teammates to their Saturday game. The boys were noisy, and Tom was getting frustrated trying to find a playing field he had never been to before. Unable to concentrate on his driving, Tom ran into another car. The accident was minor, but Tom let his frustration out in profanity.

Later that afternoon, young Michael asked his mother if his dad was a member of the Church. Michael had been taught that good

Mormons don't swear. His mother was surprised and said, "Of course your father is a Church member."

"Well, Dad may be a Mormon, but I know he is not a Cub Scout!" Michael replied.

Would someone listening to you ever think, "Well, he may be a Mormon, but he sure isn't a Christian?"[1]

As a missionary, if people watched you for one week would they say, "He or she is full of charity and faith and the Spirit of God?" Would you be considered by your very actions as being a devout Mormon? Would you be guilty of thinking of everyone before yourself? Would you be gauged as an impersonator of Christ because of your deeds? Would people call you too religious? When my son Tyler was younger, he had a friend tease him about not watching bad movies, and he called him "Mormon boy." I can think of no greater compliment to a young man striving to live the gospel. The greatest blessing we can receive for living the gospel and being full of faith is the peace and approval that comes from a loving Father in Heaven.

Paul also admonishes missionaries to be examples of the believers "in charity, in spirit, [and] in faith" (1 Timothy 4:12). I testify that if you do this you will be full of power and light. Robert Alden said, "There is not enough darkness in all the world to put out the light of even one small candle."[2] Light never comes from living a dark life. Light doesn't come from serving a dark mission. Light only comes to a young elder or sister when they live the principles of truth and light. For this reason, a righteous missionary lights up those around them through their faith and goodness.

In the Book of Mormon, we read of a politician who went to work and whose life was changed by the power and light of a true example of the believers of Christ. He witnessed a council trying a man who claimed to be a prophet and representative of God. This politician listened to the prophet's words as he spoke with power and sincerity. The prophet spoke of commandments and of the Atonement of Jesus Christ. He testified that Christ was the only means of salvation. Despite the King and the council's desires to "lay their hands on him," they could not.

For the Spirit of the Lord was upon him; and his face shone with exceeding luster, even as Moses' did while in the mount of Sinai, while speaking with the Lord.

And he spake with power and authority from God (Mosiah 13:5–6).

The politician was Alma, and the prophet was Abinadi. Abinadi was quite literally a light to Alma because of the power and spiritual light he possessed as a true and faithful representative of Christ. Abinadi's sincere words changed Alma's heart, and he was never the same again. He recognized truth and light, and he told his fellow politicians that Abinadi's character matched his message and that he should be set free. Despite the ramifications, Alma chose to be true to Abinadi's message from that day forward for the rest of his life. There is very real power and light given to those who are examples of the believers "in charity, in spirit, [and] in faith" (1 Timothy 4:12).

Finally, Paul reminds us that purity is a powerful indication of being an example of the believers. As a missionary, remember that purity brings power—power to call upon the Spirit, power to exercise faith, power in prayer, and true power to become a living disciple of Christ. There are many wonderful blessings and promises that are given to the pure. Christ promised, "And blessed are all the pure in heart, for they shall see God" (3 Nephi 12:8). My personal experiences have convinced me of a secondary principle relating to purity that is also true. Through the pure in heart, others will see God. I have seen converts, investigators, and friends truly come to know God through the charity, goodness, and faith of missionaries who are pure in heart.

Purity is one of the greatest powers we have as missionaries. Many years ago, Vernon Law (a Latter-day Saint and a man of faith and purity) played baseball for the Pittsburg Pirates. He was an example of truth and righteousness to those around him and to his teammates. His example was so good that everyone in major league baseball called him "the deacon" or "the preacher." He had a very successful baseball career and helped his team win the 1960 World Series. He was also a Cy Young Award winner, an award given to the best pitcher in baseball. In 1955, he had a unique experience during a game between the Phillies and the Pirates. A big scuffle and several intense arguments broke out between the two teams. The umpire, Stan Landes, came over and ejected Vernon from the dugout. After the game, the umpire wrote in his report, "I didn't want Vern to hear all the abusive language."[3] Those around Vernon knew that he truly lived what he believed and that he was pure.

May those around you know by your words, deeds, faith, and purity that you are a living and true example of the believers. Remember whose name you wear on your missionary name tag every day, and may you powerfully represent the Savior and His gospel.

Your friend,
Brother Jeff Erickson

NOTES

1. Robert K. Dellenbach, "Profanity," *New Era*, May 1992.

2. Robert Alden quoted in Martin H. Manser, comp., *The Westminster Collection of Christian Quotations* (Louisville, KY: Westminster John Knox, 2001), 61.

3. Scott Taylor, "Place in history: Famous HR was key, but Vern Law played a role, too," *Deseret News*, October 13, 2005.

IMPRESSIONS FROM THE HOLY GHOST

Dear Elders and Sisters,

As a bishop, the Lord taught me a critical lesson about listening to impressions. The bishopric and I were searching for a new Relief Society president. We had started with ten wonderful candidates and had narrowed it down to three. We had prayed about it, but no real answer had come. We decided to wait. I had my top choice of the three in my mind but was still waiting on the Lord. The next Sunday, as I sat on the stand during sacrament meeting, the Lord told me who the new president should be. This good sister was not even on the list of the original ten.

When I brought her into the bishop's office to extend the call, I had a remarkable experience. We had a prayer and talked for a bit and then I invited this good sister to be the new Relief Society president. She started to cry. Through her tears, she said, "I have been praying for something like this. I have felt so worthless. I am so thankful that the Lord would call me." I cried also as I saw (not for the first time) how God loves all of His children. I was so grateful for the inspiration and impression to call whom the Lord would call. This good sister was a blessing to watch over the next few years as she served so faithfully.

I want to speak about impressions and seeking the inspiration and guidance of the Holy Ghost daily. Elder Craig Christensen said, "We all have experiences with the Holy Ghost, even though we may not always recognize them. As inspired thoughts come into our minds, we know them to be true by the spiritual feelings that enter into our

Becoming a
Better Teacher

hearts. . . . The Holy Ghost is a personage of spirit who communicates to our spirits through feelings and impressions."[1]

Here are a few scriptural reminders of some of the blessings the Holy Ghost will bring to missionaries who are seeking to listen to the feelings and impressions of the Spirit.

- "And it came to pass that the voice of the Lord came unto my father, that we should arise and go down into the ship" (1 Nephi 18:5). This verse is a reminder that the Spirit will tell us when and where to go.

- "But behold, the Lord God poured in his Spirit into my soul, insomuch that I did confound him in all his words" (Jacob 7:8). As teachers, the Spirit will tell you what to say. The Spirit also will confound the proud.

- "And it came to pass that after he had poured out his whole soul to God, the voice of the Lord came to him" (Mosiah 26:14). When we are earnest in our prayers, we will receive the Spirit. We need to ask for and plead for promptings and impressions. The Lord will answer our prayers and the promptings and impressions will come.

- "Behold, I say unto you they are made known unto me by the Holy Spirit of God. Behold, I have fasted and prayed many days that I might know these things of myself. And now I do know of myself that they are true; for the Lord God hath made them manifest unto me by his Holy Spirit; and this is the spirit of revelation which is in me" (Alma 5:46). The Holy Ghost reveals truth to those who petition the Lord through fasting and prayer. As a missionary, you can plead for the Spirit to manifest the truth unto your investigators and less-actives that you work with.

- "For my soul delighteth in plainness; for after this manner doth the Lord God work among the children of men. For the Lord God giveth light unto the understanding; for he speaketh unto men according to their language, unto their understanding" (2 Nephi 31:3). The Holy Ghost will speak to you in a way that you will understand. He will tell you in simple thoughts what to do, who to pray for, where to go, or who to see on a certain day. The Holy Ghost will speak to the people you teach in a way they will understand; you don't need to fill in the gaps because the Spirit will do that.

As you can see, there are many scriptures that explain the magnificent operations of the Spirit. The lessons always seem to be similar. Fast and pray, then ask, and then ponder and listen. The impressions won't typically come as a bolt, but rather as a quiet thought or voice. Ideas and thoughts will come during your prayers. Take time to listen and receive heavenly direction. *Revelation fails when we fail to ask.* Remember Nephi's thought-provoking question to his brothers, "Have ye inquired of the Lord?" (1 Nephi 15:8). Ask daily for guidance and help. Elder Boyd K. Packer said, "Prayer is *your* personal key to heaven."[2]

With all of these wonderful promises, how can we more effectively recognize when the Holy Ghost is directing us to take specific actions? President Boyd K. Packer said, "The Holy Ghost speaks with a voice that you *feel* more than you *hear*. It is described as a 'still small voice.' And while we speak of 'listening' to the whisperings of the Spirit, most often one describes a spiritual prompting by saying, 'I had a *feeling.'* . . . If ever you receive a prompting to do something that makes you *feel* uneasy, something you know in your *mind* to be wrong and contrary to the principles of righteousness, do not respond to it!"[3]

On many occasions as a bishop, I felt blessed when the Holy Ghost would fill me with impressions as I would scan the audience from my seat on the stand. Many of these impressions were forgotten by the end of the Sabbath day. I wisely began to record these spiritual whisperings in a journal, and they soon became my "bishop to-do list" for the week. One such whispering was about a young girl in the ward who was wonderful, but was really struggling. The Spirit said, "Write her a letter." I acted on that impression. The words of the letter were filled with the Spirit, and I felt good about doing as the Lord had directed. My testimony of that impression was confirmed a few days later when her mother came to me with tears in her eyes and thanked me for the "oft-read" letter. I walked away from that exchange grateful for a loving Father who remembers all of His children.

Remember twenty-five-year-old Captain Moroni going into his first battle against an overwhelming Lamanite army. He sent men to Alma to see if he would ask God for assistance.

> . . . And Moroni, also, knowing of the prophecies of Alma, sent certain men unto him, desiring him that he should inquire of the Lord whither the armies of the Nephites should go to defend themselves against the Lamanites.
>
> And it came to pass that the word of the Lord came unto Alma, and Alma informed the messengers of Moroni. (Alma 43:23–24)

What if Moroni had never sought the help of the Spirit in the forthcoming battle? Would the outcome have been different?

Elder Richard G. Scott taught, "As each impression came, I carefully wrote it down. . . . Had I not responded to the first impressions and *recorded them*, I would not have received the last, most precious impression."[4] Elder Scott is telling us that we must respond to the impressions we receive from the Lord, and, if we don't, those impressions may not continue to come.

In 1921, Elders David O. McKay and Hugh Cannon were touring the missions of the Church around the world. They were in Hawaii and decided they would visit the Kilauea volcano one evening with a group of ten. On the rim of the volcano, bitter cold winds chilled them, while the heat of the lava nearly blistered their faces. One of the elders discovered a volcanic balcony about four feet down inside the crater where observers could look at the molten lava without being chilled by the cold wind while also being protected from the intense heat.

> After being down there in their protected spot for some time, suddenly Brother McKay said to those with him, "Brethren, I feel impressed that we should get out of here."
>
> With that he assisted the elders to climb out, and then they in turn helped him up to the wind-swept rim. It seems incredible, but almost immediately the whole balcony crumbled and fell with a roar into the molten lava a hundred feet or so below. . . .
>
> None of us who were witnesses to this experience could ever doubt the reality of "revelation in our day!" (Randal S. Chase, *Making Precious Things Plain*.[5]

I am certain that those brethren were all grateful for the impressions of a righteous man on that occasion.

Elder Craig Christensen said, "The Holy Ghost loves us and wants us to be happy."[6] Elder Christensen's thought helped me realize that as we testify to the people of our mission, the Holy Ghost wants them to be happy and is looking for opportunities to change their hearts. May we feel what the Holy Ghost would have us feel and act upon those sacred feelings as missionaries.

Your friend,
Brother Jeff Erickson

NOTES

1. Craig C. Christensen, "An Unspeakable Gift from God," *Ensign*, November 2012.
2. Boyd K. Packer, "Personal Revelation: The Gift, the Test, and the Promise," *Ensign*, November 1994; emphasis in original.
3. Ibid.; emphasis in original.
4. Richard G. Scott, "To Acquire Spiritual Guidance," *Ensign*, November 2009; emphasis added.
5. Washington, Utah: Plain and Precious Publishing, 6:308.
6. Christensen, "An Unspeakable Gift from God."

A BUILDER

Dear Elders and Sisters,

I will never forget a few years ago when I drove into my cul-de-sac and found a few barricade barriers with lights spread across the middle of the street. The barricades were wrapped with yellow caution tape between them. My first impression was that some neighborhood renegades were out having some fun. After closer inspection, I realized it wasn't a bunch of renegades at all. This prank was the work of someone who was "a builder." On one of the barriers there was a large sign which read, "Caution: gorgeous girl lives on this street." I read the sign, and I was impressed with the architect's work. It was such a grand idea that I wanted to lie and tell my wife that I had made the sign for her. I am certain there was a girl on my street that night whose spirits were lifted by some very creative and kind words—words that elevated. I was in awe that someone would go to such great lengths to lift someone's self-worth in such a wonderful way. The "monument" on my street that night was a reminder to me of how someone's life can be impacted by one who is "a builder."

One of the most insightful scriptures in the New Testament is a very simple, yet thought-provoking, verse in the book of Luke: "And there appeared an angel unto him from heaven, strengthening him" (Luke 22:43). In an overwhelming moment, Christ needed to be lifted and encouraged, and an angel was sent to strengthen Him. The angel may have reminded Him of His mission or His central role in the plan, or just simply lifted His spirits. This much is certain; that angel was an absolute blessing to our Savior at that particular moment during that sacred night.

What does it mean to build? It means to develop, shape, construct, and fabricate. When I study these words, I realize the power of building. A builder has the ability to shape and construct the character, self-worth, and self-esteem of others. I have watched many men and women who are builders shape the character of others in the Church over and over again. The following allegory demonstrates the critical differences between a builder and a destroyer:

> Two happy little critters, very similar in appearance, went to work one day at different jobs. How exciting it was to venture out into the world of work, thrift, and industry. They were both happy to have a job and contribute. They both worked hard at their craft and were busy as bees throughout the day. They both came home exhausted and tired from a long day's work.
>
> Day after day, they returned to their labors as the years came and went. Both were engaged in huge projects requiring significant effort and labor. One was engulfed in building great structures and was anxiously engaged in his work. He found great satisfaction in the completion of his projects and his role in their development and construction. How could a little critter not be a little bit proud to have participated in building such wonderful masterpieces?
>
> Meanwhile, the other little critter was a member of a demolition team that traveled the city and performed their labors. They carefully destroyed large structures and edifices that once gleamed and stood with sturdiness and majesty. At the conclusion of his work each day, he found discontent, dissatisfaction, and regret.
>
> One little critter was building castles and palaces, while the other was destroying homes and carefully designed buildings. When I look at my life, I wonder what little critter am I? Am I an ant who diligently labors and builds amazing structures, or am I a termite who is daily destroying what others have so carefully built?

At the end of Elder Neal A. Maxwell's mission, his mission president wrote a short note at the bottom of a letter to Elder Maxwell's bishop complimenting the young missionary on his work. Elder Maxwell said, "It took President Eyre thirty seconds to write this [the note], but it gave me encouragement for fifty years."[1] Like Elder Maxwell, I am grateful for those who take precious time to build those around them.

My son Talmage decided one Veterans Day to go around the house and put notes on some of his family members' bedroom doors. The yellow sticky note on my door said, "I love you, Mom. Happy Veterans Day! You too, Dad." The note to his baby sister Holland read, "Holland, you are the cutest girl in the world." To his brother Taft, he wrote, "You stink." Something that had started out so positive turned into something negative. His mom reprimanded him about the note and invited him to redirect his thoughts and comments about his brother. He was quick to repent and put a new note on Taft's door. The new note said, "Taft, you are the best brother ever." There is something wonderful that happens when you build and elevate others instead of attempting to shatter their spirits.

In this day and age, a common high school mentality seems to be: "Look at me, look what I am doing." Many social media applications seem to promote a self-centered display of one's actions, accomplishments, and triumphs. I have a son in high school that seems to defy many of those tendencies; he is a master builder. He helps others develop greater feelings of self-worth. I have witnessed him rejoice in the successes of others. I have witnessed him have hundreds of "best friends" at school. Time and time again, I have seen his friends and schoolmates light up when they see him. This past year, he was nominated for a high school popularity award given annually to a young man at his high school. Students choose about eight students from the high school, and then those who have been nominated come to participate in an event to see who becomes "Mr. Highland." After he was nominated, he turned it down for a few reasons; one of which was that he wanted someone else to have the opportunity. He didn't need that award to elevate himself, and he wanted someone else to be blessed by the opportunity and the attention.

Here is a poem I love called, "The Builder."

> I watched them tearing a building down,
> A group of men in a busy town;
> With a ho-heave-ho and a lusty yell
> They swung a beam and a sidewalk fell.
>
> I asked the foreman, "Are these men skilled,
> And the men you'd hire if you had to build?"

95

He gave a laugh and said: "No indeed!
Just common labor is all I need.

I can easily wreck in a day or two
What builders have taken a year to do!"
And I thought to myself as I went my way,
Which of these roles have I tried to play?

Am I a builder who builds with care,
Measuring life by the rule and square,
Am I shaping my deeds to a well-made plan,
Patiently does the best I can?

Or am I a wrecker, who walks the town,
Content with the labor of tearing down.[2]

One of the many blessings of a mission is the opportunity to elevate the lives of others. Missionaries lift members, investigators, less-actives, companions, other missionaries, and anyone they come in contact with. When a missionary leaves an area, it is easy to tell if he has elevated others by how they react when he departs. True emissaries of Christ are a light in a dark world. There is a wonderful truth that is similar to the golden rule; I like to call it the "principle of elevation." When you elevate others, you, in turn, are elevated also. The best synonym I have found for the word *elevation* is exaltation.[3] May we all help each other to exalt one another.

Your friend,
Brother Jeff Erickson

NOTES

1. Bruce C. Hafen, *A Disciple's Life* (Salt Lake City: Deseret Book, 2002), 148.
2. Unknown author in Samuel Norfleet Etheredge, *Poetry for a Lifetime: All-Time Favorite Poems to Delight and Inspire All Ages* (MiraVista, 2014).
3. *Merriam-Webster Thesaurus*, s.v. "elevation," accessed February 28, 2017, www.merriam-webster.com/thesaurus/elevation.

CORNER-CARRIERS

Dear Elders and Sisters,

My parents got divorced when I was fourteen. During the next few years, my good mother went to work full-time and was also enrolled in college full time. She remarkably held our family together while she truly ran faster than she had strength. During this time, I had some deep emotional and spiritual needs, and I was blessed with many tender mercies that came in the way of wonderful families and powerful people who played a pivotal role in my life. One of the families I gravitated to during my critical high school years was my bishop and his family, the Merrill's. They loved me as one of their own. Two friends and I spent hundreds of hours during our high school years in their home. We spent numerous weekend nights there. We hung out with the bishop and his wife, we played games with them, we watched movies with them, we had great lessons with them, we toilet papered their house, we played pranks on them, we shared concerns with them, and we even went on trips with them. They loved us and we loved them. On one occasion, they even put on a four-course dinner for a date and me and dressed in formal attire to serve us.

Occasionally, some of the pranks we played on the family were not well thought-out. Looking back, some of these shortsighted attempts at fun were dumb, offensive, and inappropriate. In the Merrill's home, there hung a beautiful desert mural that was about four feet high and twelve feet long. One day, my friend, thinking he was funny, drew a little snake with a sharpie in the desert landscape of the mural. It was a little hard to detect so it took them a few weeks to discover the addition to the mural. When they discovered the newly added reptile, they just laughed and thought my friend to be clever. Privately, they may have wanted to punish him or us for our shenanigans, but they somehow never did. They were quick to forgive and quick to show mercy, and they continued to love us and make us feel welcome, valued, and important. I always felt they were short on bitterness and anger and long on acceptance and praise.

I didn't know it at the time, but this good family was keeping me active in the Church, nourishing my testimony, helping me build a desire to serve a full-time mission, and inviting me to come unto Christ through their example. I knew these good people loved me because they took an interest in my life and shared in my sorrows and successes.

I have been the benefactor of many amazing people like the Merrill's who have lifted me, taught me, and mentored me in many critical junctures in my life. Without these precious people, my testimony of Jesus Christ and His gospel would not be flourishing like it is today. I like to call these people "corner-carriers." Let me explain what I mean by a corner-carrier. Mark records that Jesus Christ

> Entered into Capernaum after some days; and it was noised that he was in the house.
>
> And straightway many were gathered together, insomuch that there was no room to receive them, no, not so much as about the door: and he preached the word unto them.
>
> And they come unto him, bringing one sick of the palsy, which was borne of four. (Mark 2:1–3)

I love to visualize a scene of a full house and no room. The four individuals carrying the bed of their dear friend desperately wanted to transport their friend to the Savior. They embarked on a difficult endeavor because their friend was paralyzed and they literally carried him to Christ. The first lesson I gain from this is how desperately do we want to get our friends to the Savior? What are we willing to do in order to bring them to hear Christ, see Christ, and feel of His message and love? These four friends each carried corners of a bed to bring this man to Christ. Their motives were not selfish or designed to draw attention to themselves. Their entire objective was for this man, their friend, to come unto Christ.

The experience continues, "And when they could not come nigh unto him for the press, they uncovered the roof where he was: and when

Serving like the Savior

they had broken it up, they let down the bed wherein the sick of the palsy lay" (Mark 2:4). After much hard work, these four corner-carriers placed their friend right in front of the Savior, and "When Jesus saw their faith, he said unto the sick of the palsy, Son, thy sins be forgiven thee" (Mark 2:5). The amazing thing about this experience is that we don't even know the original feelings of the paralyzed man. We don't know if he even wanted to be carried to the house. We don't know what he knew about the Savior. The one thing we know for certain is that the four corner-carriers were filled with faith because they did everything within their power to put their friend in Christ's presence. They knew if they could somehow transfer their friend to the Savior, his life would be changed in some powerful manner.

After hearing the Savior forgive the paralyzed man, the scribes immediately began claiming that it was blasphemy for Christ to forgive sins. His response was powerful:

> And immediately when Jesus perceived in his spirit that they so reasoned within themselves, he said unto them, Why reason ye these things in your hearts?
>
> Whether is it easier to say to the sick of the palsy, Thy sins be forgiven thee; or to say, Arise, and take up thy bed, and walk?
>
> But that ye may know that the Son of man hath power on earth to forgive sins, (he saith to the sick of the palsy)
>
> I say unto thee, Arise, and take up thy bed, and go thy way into thine house.
>
> And immediately he arose, took up the bed, and went forth before them all; insomuch that they were all amazed, and glorified God, saying, We never saw it on this fashion. (Mark 2:8–12)

I can't help but wonder, *what if these four corner-carriers hadn't brought their friend to the Savior that day? What if they were too busy to bring their friend to Christ? What if they would have said, "it will be too hard to get him to the Savior?"*

Every full-time missionary is a corner-carrier. As missionaries assist others on their journeys to Jesus Christ, they are able to watch the Atonement work miracles and wonders. God needs emissaries to testify of Christ and to assist individuals who are coming to Christ. These faithful servants know that every instance of spiritual palsy can be healed through the miracle of the Atonement. The example of these

Serving like the Savior

four consecrated brethren teaches us powerful principles about what it means to carry corners.

First, corner-carriers are full of faith. These ministers never doubted that their friend would have an amazing experience when he met Christ. They knew their mission to get this man to Christ would be difficult, but they knew it would be worth it. Remember, it was "when Jesus saw their faith" that the miracle occurred (Mark 2:5). May you as a missionary be filled with faith as you carry the people you serve to Christ.

Second, the mission of a corner-carrier is not easy. It takes sacrifice, prayer, endurance, and discernment. It takes obedience, creativity, effort, and perseverance. At any point, one of the four could have said, "This is too difficult; it is not going to work." I am impressed that none of them shared those sentiments; they simply endured with faith through the difficulty of the situation. These individuals overcame every obstacle in their path to get their friend to the Savior.

Third, corner-carriers work together. One man carrying a corner of the bed would not have succeeded. He needed companions; he needed others to help with the heavy load. Corner-carriers work with others consecrated to do the work of God. Missionaries who carry corners work with mission leaders, ward and branch leaders, local members, companions, and even part-members to help others come to Christ. The work of bringing others to Christ cannot be accomplished by one corner alone. A corner-carrier realizes that every corner of the bed must be effectively carried or the success of the sacred experience is in jeopardy.

Fourth, some corners are heavier than others when doing the Lord's work. Mission presidents carry heavy corners. Trainers and assistants may carry heavy corners. You must know that if your corner is currently a little lighter, savor the moment and strengthen other's feeble knees. There will be times in your mission when your corner is heavier. Pray for the strength to bear your burden. Never be upset that you are or are not carrying the heaviest corner. A true corner-carrier will do his part when the load is light or when the load is heavy. A corner-carrier will always be grateful that he is not carrying the bed or burden alone.

Fifth, it is never about who is carrying the bed. The individuals in Mark's account had one goal in mind: get our friend to the Savior.

Serving like
the Savior

There were no thoughts of *who will get the credit when we are done? Who will enter the house first? Who will the Savior see do the most work?* True corner-carriers don't care how heavy the bed is or how heavy their corner is, they just want to get the soul in the bed to the Savior. Their joy comes from the result of seeing someone they love embrace and taste of the goodness of God. Christ is the end goal of every true corner-carrier.

May you be filled with faith as you carry others to Christ by faithfully carrying your corner.

Your friend,
Brother Jeff Erickson

Serving like
the Savior

RESCUING

Dear Elders and Sisters,

I hope this letter finds you happy and successful in your labors. I hope you are increasing your efforts to, as President Monson said, "rescue and to save."[1] What a great blessing to be full-time rescuers. I am impressed that President Monson's biography is called *To the Rescue.* What a great compliment to him. I want to cover the topic of rescuing today. I have a best friend who was spiritually rescued this year and who has returned to regular Church activity. These rescue efforts were not by me, but by some other wonderful people in his ward that reached out to him. He was reactivated, and his wife was baptized. For years, I have wanted to see him return to the Church, but I actually did very little to help. My excuse was that he was very far away (he lives a few states away). My excuse is terribly weak, but thank goodness others didn't make the same lame excuse. I could have done so much more. I don't say this out of guilt, but with a resolve to do more in the future. I believe the words Alma said to his son Corianton, "Behold, I say unto you, is not a soul at this time as precious unto God as a soul will be at the time of his coming?" (Alma 39:17).

A few months ago, I read a story of a sixty-six-year-old man named Steve in Florida who had a small terrier dog named Bounce. He called Bounce his best friend. One day, Steve was hanging out in his backyard in Orlando with Bounce. His little dog wandered close to the edge of a nearby pond. He heard his dog yelping, and he looked and saw an alligator carrying little Bounce in its mouth. He yelled, "You're not going to get her!" He ran toward the pond and leapt on top of the alligator. A wrestling match ensued in the 3-foot-deep pond, and the 7-foot, 130-pound gator tried to pin Steve to the bottom of the pond.

Eventually, Steve prevailed, freed Bounce, and threw the gator back in the pond. Both Steve and Bounce sustained injuries, but were okay after a few stitches. Steve's friends gave him a superhero cape and an alligator belt buckle after his act of heroism. In the article, Steve's closing comment was powerful. He said, "If I hesitated, I would have lost my best friend."[2]

I read Steve's story and thought, *what courage.* I also thought, "If someone would do that for a dog, why wouldn't they do that for other friends?" I looked at my life and asked myself if I am helping to free my loved ones from the clutches of the adversary. I have witnessed so many friends in my life who have succumbed to sin and have been taken captive by the habits of the flesh who need to be rescued or freed. I have tried, in some instances, to rescue these friends, but I want to do better and do more to free them from their entrapments.

A few years ago, four-year-old Baylor Andersen and his family's car slid off a highway into an icy river. They were trapped inside the car. Baylor was rescued by a man who dove into the icy water, with a group of strangers, to save him. This group of strangers, a half-dozen men, charged into the river and flipped over the car to rescue Baylor, his sister Mia, and a friend Kenya. A trooper on the scene suggested that the car must have weighed at least four thousand pounds. His father said, "I felt strongly that we had great help from the people who were there at the scene, but we also had help, I think, from some other forces."

Kenya was the only one conscious when they pulled the three from the car—Baylor and Mia were rendered unconscious by the crash. A man carried Baylor from the river and threw his limp body into the arms of a man, Buzzy Mullahkhel, who had arrived just in time to see the men flip the car over. The man carrying Baylor said, "I can't feel him for a pulse, because I can't feel my hands." "Baylor's skin was wet, cold and gray; there was no pulse, not even a faint one." Buzzy turned to the woman next to him and said, "Please tell me you know CPR." All three children were saved. Their rescue took place because these wonderful strangers risked their lives and health to save others. Their father, Roger Andersen, was so grateful for their willingness to help. He choked up as he watched his son play two days later as if nothing had ever happened. Something that could have been so tragic was turned into one of the greatest miracles Roger Andersen will ever see in his life.[3]

There is power in giving our time, talents, and energy to rescue others. A spiritual rescue is even more eternally significant than rescuing someone physically. When someone is saved from temporal death, there is usually significant gratitude. If that's the case for rescue from physical death, then what is owed to the people who save others from a certain spiritual death? What do you say to someone who saves you from the chains of the adversary, and from certain eternal destruction? How do you tell those people you are grateful?

I know it is always the Savior that truly does all the saving. How do we express our gratitude when He pulls us from the waters of spiritual death? What do we say when we rid ourselves of the burdens of sin that are drowning us? What do we say when He lifts us to levels of peace and happiness higher than we deserve? We express our gratitude by our sincere repentance, faith, and obedience. We then also have a responsibility to become instruments in His hands, and, as instruments in His hands, we also need to become rescuers.

What a blessing to be servants of God and to be called to rescue people from a world of sin, darkness, captivity, and devastation. What a blessing to have the opportunity to carry a beacon of hope to the people of the world. How wonderful to carry a life-preserving buoy that you can throw to others to save them from the depths of eternal misery, if they will but cling to it. I testify that Christ has rescued us, and we just need to reach for and hold onto his rescue buoy, which is the Atonement. This year may we all enjoy the blessings of rescuing our Father's children.

Your friend,
Brother Jeff Erickson

NOTES

1. Thomas S. Monson, "Our Responsibility to Rescue," *Ensign*, October 2013.
2. Eric Pfeiffer, "Florida grandfather wrestles gator to save pet dog," *Yahoo! News*, September 19, 2012.
3. Eric Alberty, "Utah children rescued from icy river doing well," *The Salt Lake Tribune*, January 3, 2012.

Serving like the Savior (side margin)

NOURISH

Dear Elders and Sisters,

I came across a verse in Mosiah that I would like to share some thoughts about today: "Therefore they did watch over their people, and did nourish them with things pertaining to righteousness" (Mosiah 23:18). This verse could be used to summarize the role of a missionary in their area, zone, ward or branch, and amongst the people not of our faith in their area. I believe, as full-time missionaries, you are to nourish the people with things pertaining to righteousness. What does that mean?

Last year, I read of a wonderful grandmother attempting to nourish her grandson with things pertaining to righteousness. She sent him a text encouraging him to be better than he was presently being. She said, "Stop cussing so much, They be showing [sic] you when you do."[1] This powerful text was sent to Kevin Durant—one of the best basketball players in the world—by his grandma. This good lady was inviting Kevin to be a little better, a little more righteous.

Let's start with the word *nourish*. What does it mean to nourish? I think it means to feed, to encourage, to support, to push, to help, to promote, to persuade, to influence, to convince, to sway, to give confidence, to give hope, to urge to inspired action. I love the breadth and depth of that word. The question is, are we truly nourishing others with things pertaining to righteousness? Are we encouraging others to live the gospel? We can do this with our thoughts, words, deeds, and prayers. Do people see us as a light on a hill? Are we promoting wonderful principles that are full of light and truth through our actions, examples, and lifestyle choices? Are we exact in our obedience? Are we quick to observe? Do we bring confidence to the local ward because of our exceeding faith in Christ? Do the members feel this from you: "My mouth shall speak the praise of the Lord: and let all flesh bless his holy name forever and ever" (Psalm 145:21)? Do we share faith-promoting experiences with the local members so they know God is at the helm?

A few years ago, my wife and I invited a friend, Sandra, and her two children to church with our family. Despite the distance of over thirty miles and a forty-five-minute drive, she would get up early (early enough to make an 8:00 a.m. sacrament meeting) and come to church every Sunday with our family. There was a meetinghouse less than ten minutes from her home that she could have gone to, but, for a few weeks, she made the long drive. One day, she saw the painting *Woman at the Well*, and she then explained to me why she made the long drive and attended our worship services. I will never forget her powerful thoughts. She said, "You see that picture? That is me. That is how I feel. When I come here to church, I somehow feel like the woman coming to the well with Christ, and I leave church having been filled." Her simple statements of faith were a powerful testimony to me of what a blessing it is to anyone to be "nourished with things pertaining to righteousness" (Mosiah 23:18). She and her two children began attending in her own area and were baptized a few weeks later.

Do we promote increased missionary efforts because of our desire and our invitations to the members? Here is a promise that I love: "And at all times, and in all places, he shall open his mouth and declare my gospel as with the voice of a trump, both day and night. And I will give unto him strength such as is not known among men" (D&C 24:12). There is power in opening your mouth and extending invitations. The members should be a huge part of your teaching, reactivating, and baptizing.

Is our testimony growing to the point where we feel like the sons of Mosiah? "Now they were desirous that salvation should be declared to every creature, for they could not bear that any human soul should perish; yea, even the very thoughts that any soul should endure endless torment did cause them to quake and tremble" (Mosiah 28:3). Are we urging the members to help every human soul they possibly can? Is our desire to share our testimony with others burning in us like it did in Jeremiah, who stated, "Then I said, I will not make mention of him, nor speak any more in his name. But his word was in mine heart as a burning fire shut up in my bones, and I was weary with forbearing, and I could not stay" (Jeremiah 20:9)? Are we bringing hope in Christ to those who are so desperate for light and truth in their lives?

The miracle of nourishing is found in these two principles: "And the King shall answer and say unto them, Verily I say unto you, Inasmuch as ye have done it unto one of the least of these my brethren, ye have done it unto me" (Matthew 25:40). When you nourish others, you are truly serving Christ. "Therefore all things whatsoever ye would that men should do to you, do ye even so to them: for this is the law and the prophets" (Matthew 7:12). Here is the miracle of nourishment. When you nourish others, Christ will, in turn, nourish you. I pray that you will continue to be nourished as you continue to nourish others.

Your friend,
Brother Jeff Erickson

Serving like
the Savior

NOTES

1. Jesse Dorsey, "Kevin Durant Gets Hilarious Text from Grandma: 'Stop Cussing So Much,'" *Bleacher Report*, January 15, 2013.

ADVERSITY

Dear Elders and Sisters,

A few years ago, my son Tyler was extremely sick. He came to me in the midst of feeling miserable and said, "Dad, I need you to give me your very, very strongest blessing." Tyler had already learned from prior priesthood blessings that adversity can make you stronger, and he continued, "Dad, I don't want Heavenly Father to make me strong anymore. I am just not ready to be that strong yet." I believe there are many days when we all feel what Tyler felt as a young man—that we are simply not ready for certain trials or adversities in the moment.

I want to address adversity today, because, as Elder Joseph B. Wirthlin said, "The way we react to adversity can be a major factor in how happy and successful we can be in life."[1] The Bible teaches us great things about adversity, but modern revelation enhances and deepens our understanding of why we have adversity, its role in our eternal salvation, and its limitations. Elder Wirthlin said, "If we approach adversities wisely, our hardest times can be times of greatest growth, which in turn can lead toward times of greatest happiness."[2] I know that this applies to a full-time mission because there is so much adversity, but great peace and happiness will always result from the growth we see as we faithfully serve Heavenly Father.

I hope you never have to reference this letter on your mission, but if you have to reference it many times, it means you are mortal and normal. We all have tough times, and we all get hit with adversity. We all get the adversary in our head, where he tries to thwart our efforts and make us miserable. I want to share a few principles from the gospel of Jesus Christ that will help you when adversity strikes you as a missionary. These principles will help when you lose a great investigator, when you get sick, when you get a lazy companion, and anytime you're struggling. Hopefully, some of these principles will lift you through those trying times.

First, it won't last forever. "My son, peace be unto thy soul; thine adversity and thine afflictions shall be but a small moment" (D&C 121:7). What does a small moment mean? It means, as a missionary, things will always get better tomorrow or next week or next month. Thing will get better when you meet the next wonderful investigator, when you feel well again, when a bad companion gets inspired through love, when a transfer comes, or when you get over any small hurdle you may be facing. The promise with adversity is that there is a limitation to it, and adversity will not last forever. There are some trials that last until death, but most of our adversities are limited to a small moment. As a missionary, I always found that to be the case. Some days were longer and some trials were more painful, but every hardship is eventually swallowed up in the joy of Christ. Unfortunately, the Lord has never defined the exact time involved in "a small moment."

Second, adversity will make you stronger and wiser. "If thou faint in the day of adversity, thy strength is small" (Proverbs 24:10). The design of adversity is to make us stronger. It is the refiner's fire that purifies us. Think of impure gold; as it is heated, it is refined and the impurities are burned off. When the process is complete, the gold is stronger and its beauty is magnified. The Lord said, "I will try you and prove you herewith" (D&C 98:12). May you as a missionary become as polished gold.

Third, the Lord gives weaknesses so we can rely on Him to turn them to strengths. Moroni speaks "somewhat concerning these things" and testifies that, "I would show unto the world that faith is things which are hoped for and not seen; wherefore, dispute not because ye see not, for ye receive no witness until after the trial of your faith" (Ether 12:6). Receive a witness of what? The witness that we receive is a witness that God is the author of faith, miracles, hope, love, opportunity, and strength. When our faith is tried and we endure well, God shows us great things. The Lord has promised, "And if men come unto me I will show unto them their weakness. I give unto men weakness that they may be humble; and my grace is sufficient for all men that humble themselves before me; for if

For Times of Trial

they humble themselves before me, and have faith in me, then will I make weak things become strong unto them" (Ether 12:27). Again, adversity will make weak elders and sisters strong.

Fourth, adversity is a master teacher. As a child learns to speak, they have thousands of different word choices. When my son Talmage was learning to speak, his first discernible word was "Ouch." Think of this: out of thousands of words, he seemed to learn of pain first. The pain of life can truly be a master teacher if we allow it to be. The Lord said, "And if thou shouldst be cast into the pit, or into the hands of murderers, and the sentence of death passed upon thee; if thou be cast into the deep; if the billowing surge conspire against thee; if fierce winds become thine enemy; if the heavens gather blackness, and all the elements combine to hedge up the way; and above all, if the very jaws of hell shall gape open the mouth wide after thee, know thou, my son, that all these things shall give thee experience, and shall be for thy good" (D&C 122:7).

It doesn't feel good, but the Lord says it will be for our good, and I know that is true. What does it teach us? "And not only so, but we glory in tribulations also: knowing that tribulation worketh patience" (Romans 5:3). Paul tells us that adversity teaches us patience. You can list all the attributes of Christ then, for that is what adversity will teach us. It will teach us to become like Him.

Fifth, adversity comes with great blessings to those that endure it well. In the Doctrine and Covenants, we are promised, "And then, if thou endure it well, God shall exalt thee on high; thou shalt triumph over all thy foes" (D&C 121:8). This is yet another promise echoed over and over again in the scriptures. Here are a few of those scriptural echoes:

- "Therefore, hold on thy way, and the priesthood shall remain with thee; for their bounds are set, they cannot pass. Thy days are known, and thy years shall not be numbered less; therefore, fear not what man can do, for God shall be with you forever and ever" (D&C 122:9).

- "Nevertheless, after much tribulation, the Lord did hear my cries, and did answer my prayers, and has made me an instrument in his hands in bringing so many of you to a knowledge of his truth" (Mosiah 23:10).

- "For verily I say unto you, blessed is he that keepeth my commandments, whether in life or in death; and he that is faithful in tribulation, the reward of the same is greater in the kingdom of heaven" (D&C 58:2).

- "For after much tribulation, as I have said unto you in a former commandment, cometh the blessing" (D&C 103:12).

The Lord is clear; when we endure faithfully, every promise will be kept, and we will be drenched in the blessings of heaven.

Sixth, God will protect, strengthen, and deliver us. Our Heavenly Father is aware of our trials, and He will not forsake us. Let us have the faith to say, "I will be glad and rejoice in thy mercy: for thou hast considered my trouble; thou hast known my soul in adversities." (Psalms 31:7). As you learn to rely on the Lord through your adversity, may you echo these powerful words: "And I have been supported under trials and troubles of every kind, yea, and in all manner of afflictions; yea, God has delivered me from prison, and from bonds, and from death; yea, and I do put my trust in him, and he will still deliver me" (Alma 36:27).

I will close with two of powerful verses of scripture:

"And now my son, Shiblon, I would that ye should remember, that as much as ye shall put your trust in God even so much ye shall be delivered out of your trials, and your troubles, and your afflictions, and ye shall be lifted up at the last day" (Alma 38:5).

"These things I have spoken unto you, that in me ye might have peace. In the world ye shall have tribulation: but be of good cheer; I have overcome the world" (John 16:33).

When you come to those adverse moments in your mission, be of good cheer, know that Christ will deliver you out of those trials, and that He can do so because He has overcome and endured all things. Adversity is weighty, but full of great opportunity; make the most of the adverse times in your mission.

Your friend,
Brother Jeff Erickson

For Times
of Trial

NOTES

1. Joseph B. Wirthlin, "Come What May, and Love It," *Ensign*, November 2008.
2. Ibid.

For Times
of Trial

HARD THINGS

Dear Elders and Sisters,

A few years ago, I was challenged by a friend to run a marathon with him. I had never done it before, nor did I ever want to do it. I am not a runner or jogger by nature, and probably had never run more than six miles at any given time in my life. I accepted the challenge, and we began an attempt to conquer a hard thing. We chose a four-month marathon-training regimen we found on the Internet. The regimen was very difficult; it challenged us to run every other day with a long run on Saturdays. These runs usually totaled anywhere from twenty to fifty miles per week. A few weeks before the marathon, the training regimen had us doing some daily runs as long as eighteen to twenty-two miles.

On the day of the race, I still had never run a marathon, but I now believed that I could do it. I had prepared and improved and overcome many obstacles that had stood in my way just four months earlier. I ran the race, still hit the proverbial wall, but finished the race, running faster miles than in my training times. This hard thing, running a marathon, had now been conquered. The process and the race were extremely taxing and difficult, but the reward of completing the marathon was wonderful. Looking back, it was worth the sacrifice, the training, the time, and the commitment.

Life is full of hard things. If done well, a mission is one of the hardest things you will ever do in your lifetime. If a young man or young woman can serve a faithful mission, they can do anything. I know as you serve faithfully and work hard during your mission, you will come to clearly see that, "I can do all things through Christ which strengtheneth me" (Philippians 4:13).

There is a powerful reference and lesson early on in the Book of Mormon regarding hard things:

> Wherefore, the Lord hath commanded me that thou and thy brothers should go unto the house of Laban, and seek the records, and bring them down hither into the wilderness.
>
> And now, behold thy brother's murmur, saying it is a hard thing which I have required of them; but behold I have not required it of them, but it is a commandment of the Lord.
>
> Therefore go, my son, and thou shalt be favored of the Lord, because thou hast not murmured. (1 Nephi 3:4–6)

I love those doctrinal insights regarding "hard things." The Lord challenged Lehi and his family to obey and do some things that were extremely challenging, but that would take them to a land of promise and bring them His richest blessings. These "hard things" weren't your everyday rituals of reading your scriptures for ten minutes, saying your prayers morning and night, helping a neighbor move for an hour or two, doing the dishes, or being nicer to your sister. These were serious faith-taxing requests given to a group that needed to develop greater faith for their journey ahead.

Think of the stretching the Lord was asking them to do: leave your comfortable home and possessions, go and live in a tent in the wilderness, return to Jerusalem and risk your life to get the plates, return again to Jerusalem to get Ishmael and his family, build a ship, and then embark on a long journey to an unknown destination. These things were all hard, but the Lord—as He always does with obedience—promised great blessings if they would obey.

The parallel I would like to draw between this story and your mission is how completely different Nephi and his brothers' experiences were, yet they were all called to go on the same mission. They were all sent away from their home to go a foreign land, not knowing where they would live or what to expect. The mission assignment was the same for all of them, but their approaches and their results were completely different for each of them. They were each sent out with individual strengths, weaknesses, and challenges, and they all finished their journey with the attributes and qualities that they developed during their mission to the promised land.

First, let's look at Laman and Lemuel. They were able to extract every negative view from every difficult experience they had during their journey to the promised land. When they completed their mission assignment, the attitudes, beliefs and values they had developed carried over into the rest of their lives. Their approach on their mission really was a model of the rest of their lives. They struggled with murmuring, negative attitudes, disobedience, respect, resentment, pride, understanding the things of God, sustaining priesthood authority, application of faith, and numerous other difficulties because of their approach to their mission assignment and the decisions they made in the process. They hardened their hearts, stiffened their necks, blinded their eyes, and rebelled. They were contentious, rude, and disrespectful. Their mission experience, which could have been faith promoting, somehow became overwhelmingly negative, discouraging, and miserable. Why? There are a few reasons, but in this letter I want to focus on the doctrine of the blessings that come from conquering "hard things."

Laman and Lemuel never fully understood two important principles regarding obedience to God when asked to do hard things. The first of these two principles is that the miracle of accomplishing difficult things is found in knowing that "the Lord giveth no commandments unto the children of men, save he shall prepare a way for them that they may accomplish the thing which he commandeth them" (1 Nephi 3:7). The second is that "Our most significant opportunities will be found in times of greatest difficulty."[1]

I love to cook breakfast for my kids. I have become a connoisseur of fine breakfast foods and of cookware. I have used many types of pans over the years to cook eggs, burritos, sausage links, pieces of bacon, vegetables, slices of ham, hash browns, pancakes, and many other foods. I have learned a hard lesson over and over again. Most non-stick frying pans are still difficult to clean and foods still stick to them. I like to cook without butter or oil, which makes it even tougher with sticky foods that want to attach to the surface of the supposedly non-stick pans.

There is a specific type of pan my wife bought about a year ago that I love. When she bought it I was upset because she said, "You must wash it by hand because if you throw it in the dishwasher it will ruin the cooking surface." I immediately thought this was a waste of time

For Times of Trial

because I believed that every pan should just be placed in the dishwasher. We had never had a non-stick pan that worked for very long, so I felt that washing a frying pan by hand was a lot of extra work just to preserve a surface that wouldn't remain non-stick. But, I soon learned that if we did the extra work and washed the pan by hand, the surface remained in its original state, which was truly non-stick. It was harder to care for this piece of cookware, since it required hand scrubbing and hand drying. The extra effort was rewarded though, because it made cooking without oil easier, less messy, and it reduced the need to scrape the pan. Although it was more difficult to care for these pans, I soon observed the wisdom and the value in doing so. Like the pans, which required more work, life is full of hard things that require hard work. When we put effort into these more difficult tasks, we will have greater experiences as a result.

Nephi and Sam gleaned from their trying experiences an appreciation and recognition of the goodness of God. (See 2 Nephi 26:33.) They were able to find life lessons in their experiences. They were able to feel the spirit of their mission, and they were able to build faith through the refining of their souls. They were humble, contrite, confident, and converted. They were able, even through agonizing adversity, to see and feel the "tender mercies" of the Lord (1 Nephi 1:20). They were able to become reliant on the Lord, knowing that He would provide. What made them different from their brothers? One common thread seems to be their recognition that hard things were a critical part of the plan of God. Their approach and determination to do hard things seemed to define who they became.

When Nephi was asked by the Lord to build the boat, his brothers laughed because they knew the project would be too hard for young Nephi to accomplish. Nephi's approach to hard things is demonstrated in his response to the Lord. He did not ask why, he simply asked, "Where do I go to get what I need?" (See 1 Nephi 17:9.) With Nephi's determination, courage, and, most importantly, faith, the boat project commenced. In a short time, even Laman and Lemuel were participating in building the boat. It seemed to be that building the boat was the only time that Laman and Lemuel didn't complain. Even the most reluctant of missionaries can get caught up in the hard work of building something directed and designed by the Lord. As missionaries,

For Times
of Trial

117

may you get caught up in the cause of Christ, may you put your trials and barriers in the rearview mirror and press forward with steadfastness in Christ. Every missionary can do hard things because God will give you the strength to perform them.

The Lord gave a powerful warning about upcoming difficulties to David Whitmer when he was shown the golden plates. "Even though he was one of the three witnesses to the Book of Mormon, he lost the Spirit and was excommunicated from the Church in 1838. Although he never denied his testimony of the Book of Mormon, he was a constant critic of Joseph Smith and died outside the church. We note with particular interest that when Moroni showed the three witnesses the plates, he turned directly to David Whitmer and said, 'David, blessed is he that endureth to the end.'"[2] We would do well to heed Moroni's exhortation, since we know hard things are upon us as missionaries defending those sacred plates.

I look back at my mission life and recall so many great lessons learned when my companions and I did hard things. Thank goodness for a loving Father that understands that true growth comes when our faith is challenged and we are truly tested. May you press forward with steadfastness in Christ as you approach the hard things in your daily mission service.

Your friend,
Brother Jeff Erickson

For Times of Trial

NOTES

1. Thomas S. Monson, "Meeting Your Goliath," *New Era*, June 2008.
2. Joseph Fielding McConkie and Craig J. Ostler, *Revelations of the Restoration* (Salt Lake City: Deseret Book, 2000), 124.

BITTER CUPS

Dear Elders and Sisters,

I have a few thoughts I wanted to share with you about bitter cups. You might have many questions about them. What is a bitter cup? Why must we have bitter cups? Why are they so bitter? What do I do when I have to drink from a bitter cup?

A bitter cup is what Nephi called "a hard thing" (1 Nephi 3:5). A bitter cup can be a trial you do not always request or deserve. A bitter cup is something that will test you to the very core. A bitter cup is usually something you don't want, but despite that, God finds it necessary to give you. A bitter cup is so intense that it bends, breaks, bows, and finally beautifies your soul.

The Savior, reflecting back on the Atonement, said, "Which suffering caused myself, even God, the greatest of all, to tremble because of pain, and to bleed at every pore, and to suffer both body and spirit—and would that I might not drink the bitter cup, and shrink" (D&C 19:18). The Savior called the most difficult moment of His earthly existence a bitter cup. The Savior had a choice to make during His biggest tribulation: does He drink from the bitter cup even though He doesn't have to—even though all the sins of the world aren't His own?

The Savior was in the midst of completing the hardest task of His life; the pain was excruciating beyond our comprehension, and the weight of it was crushing—to the point that blood was literally compressed from every pore. Could He do it? Yes. God wouldn't ask Him to do something He could not do. A second question was *should* He do it? The answer is easy for us to give, since we know that the entire plan rested on His decision to become the Savior of the world. He knew He *should* do it, but then came the question, *would* He do it? Even for the Savior in His most bitter moment, He faced the question we all face:

will you drink this bitter cup? The same question holds true for all of us when we are faced with our lesser bitter cups. The lingering eternal question really is: do we drink or shrink? God has answered the other questions for us. Yes, we *can* do it, and yes, we *should* do it, but *will* we do it?

There is power in knowing the Savior drank the most bitter and all-encompassing cup. One of the lessons we learn from His Atonement is that we, too, can drink the bitter cup because He did it for us. One of the purposes of the Atonement is to teach us that with God, anything is possible. Through the Savior's drinking of the bitterest cup, we, too, have power to drink from our own bitter cups.

In this context, *to shrink* means to cower away from something because we feel it is too difficult. To shrink also means we withdraw from God and the Spirit. It means we lose our courage to act, while shying away from things that are uncomfortable, demanding, and difficult. To shrink is to fall back to who or where we were before we knew God. Shrink is a word of weakness, frailty, fear, and cowardice. To shrink also means to be without power—thus, without power in the priesthood. Shrinking results in a failure to accomplish worthy goals and objectives because we are without the faith to do so.

Recently, three of my sons were asked to do a certain workout twice a week that was very difficult. It was not convenient for them and the results wouldn't be seen for some time, but they were promised significant results in the future. The workout plan was much harder than any other training or workout they had done in the past. Should they accept the challenge, the promise was that they would increase in strength and speed. One son opted out saying, "It's just not for me." What wasn't for him? Nothing in that workout would harm him or be detrimental to his goals and desires. All the benefits of the workout would have been a blessing to him in his fitness and sporting goals. The real question for him was, "Drink or shrink?" Yes, he *could* do it, and yes, he *should* do it, but *would* he do it? In this instance, he chose to shrink. The benefits continued to come for the other two boys doing their workouts. Again, do we drink or shrink?

In order to find the motivation necessary to drink rather than shrink from our bitter cups, we need to know: *why bitter cups*? The Savior answers this question when He speaks to the Nephites. The

Savior said, "I am the light and the life of the world; and I have drunk out of that bitter cup *which the Father hath given me*" (3 Nephi 11:11; emphasis added). God gives us bitter cups! Why would He do that to His children that He loves? Because bitter cups are the only way to *become* more than we are now. Mormon said, "Nevertheless the Lord seeth fit to chasten his people; yea he trieth their patience and their faith" (Mosiah 23:21). Paul also said, "For whom the Lord loveth he chasteneth" (Hebrews 12:6). Bitter cups are truly part of the great and merciful plan.

What is currently your bitter cup? Remember, a loving God will not give you a task that is too hard for you to accomplish. He just doesn't work that way. So, *can* you drink it? Yes! *Should* you drink it? Yes! *Will* you drink it? That answer is entirely up to you.

When you drink the bitter cup, as your body and soul digest the contents, you change. The contents stir within you the ability to create something majestic, powerful, and inspiring. The contents give you strength through faith in Christ and cause you to have "faith, hope, charity, and love with an eye single to the glory of God" (D&C 4:5); they cause you to "remember faith, virtue, knowledge, temperance, patience, brotherly kindness, godliness, charity, humility, diligence" (D&C 4:6).

Remember Nephi's inspired question to his brothers: "Is there anything too hard for the Lord?" (See 1 Nephi 4:1–3.) The answer really is *there is not*. The Lord can help you overcome, accomplish, and endure anything. The Lord can help you *be* anything. The Lord can help you become spiritually healthy and be the best missionary you possibly can be, but He only can do this if you will drink the bitter cup!

A mission will make you a better person, a better son or daughter, a better brother or sister, a better father or mother, and a better husband or wife. Because of a mission, you will lead a better life and, most importantly, you will lead a celestial life. Your mission has been designed specifically for you. As you drink the bitter cup of an entire mission, you will soon realize how sweet and delicious the results are. This bitter cup contains what you need; the Lord has prepared it just for you. I challenge you to have the faith to drink and not shrink! I know the Lord will do the rest.

Your friend,
Brother Jeff Erickson

For Times
of Trial

DIGGING DEEP: THE EXTRA MILE

Dear Elders and Sisters,

Today I want to write about doing more as a missionary. President Hinckley challenged, "I want to urge you to stand a little taller, to rise a little higher, to be a little better."[1] The Savior invited, "And whosoever shall compel thee to go a mile, go with him twain" (Matthew 5:41). Elder James E. Faust said, "At times all of us are called upon to stretch ourselves and do more than we think we can. I'm reminded of President Theodore Roosevelt's quip, 'I am only an average man but, by George, I work harder at it than the average man.'"[2]

A mission requires that we stretch beyond our normal capacities and do just a little more than we thought we could, or more than we have in the past. I found as a missionary that even a little extra effort, a little more love, a little more optimism, a little more pondering, a little more obedience, and a little more fervent prayer invited a little more of the Spirit and more blessings. "Some of the most rewarding times of our lives are those 'extra mile' hours given in service when the body says it wants to relax, but our better self emerges and says, 'Here am I; send me.'"[3]

Every missionary should do their personal best. "The athlete with the greatest desire to succeed will stand a greater chance of reaching his or her goal. The same holds true for the student or the musician or whatever it is that you young men [and women] aspire to be. A five-year study of many of the United States' top athletes, musicians, and scholars has recently concluded that 'drive and determination, not great natural talent, led to their extraordinary success.'"[4] Furthermore, "In whatever you want to improve upon, whether it be schoolwork,

123

athletics, music, or studying the scriptures, just give a little extra—every day. Fifteen minutes a day for one year adds up to over ninety-one hours."[5]

The easiest route is not the extra-mile route, but that extra mile is the most rewarding mile. One night, as my family was cleaning up after dinner, my wife was trying to have all the kids pick up some things around the house. In her efforts to motivate, she said to our son Taft, "I need you to go the extra mile." Taft cried out loudly, "No! Not the extra mile!" The extra mile does take heart, and it ultimately requires us to utilize the additional strength that can come from the Atonement of Jesus Christ.

There is a powerful story told in the Old Testament about the Syrian army led by Benhadad, king of Syria. He had laid siege to Samaria in Israel. His armies had surrounded the city, and they would not let any food into the city. Conditions in Samaria were awful as there was no food. Mothers were boiling and eating their own children, and the head of a donkey sold for eighty pieces of silver. These were dire times for the people of Samaria, and there seemed to be no way out of these intolerable conditions except to surrender and face certain death. (See 2 Kings 6.) Outside the walls of Samaria, there were four lepers; their flesh was being eaten away by disease and they were starving. They had been content to do little to change their fate or their destiny. They posed this powerful question, which is the question I wish to address: "Why sit we here until we die?" (2 Kings 7:3). What a great question for all of us—why are we resting? Why are we sitting? Why are we waiting? Why are we not doing more? Why are we not going the extra mile? Why don't we do something to better our situation? Why don't we go and do?

The lepers then said, "If we say, we will enter into the city, then the famine is in the city, and we shall die there: and if we sit still here, we die also. Now therefore come, and let us fall unto the host of the Syrians: if they save us alive, we shall live; and if they kill us, we shall but die" (2 Kings 7:4). The lepers reasoned that, in Samaria they would probably starve, but in the camp of the Syrians they might get some food, and then if the Syrians killed them, they were going to die anyway. They decided to take action, and so they locked arms and marched toward the Syrian army. (See 2 Kings 7:5.)

Diligence Is Key

Meanwhile, unbeknownst to the lepers, Elisha had spoken. He had prophesied that on this day in Samaria there would be an abundance of good, but he didn't say how. In fulfillment of this prophecy, as these men made their way to Syria, the Lord sent a noise with them.

> For the Lord had the host of the Syrians to hear a noise of chariots, and a noise of horses, even the noise of a great host: and they said one to another, Lo, the king of Israel hath hired against us the kings of the Hittites, and the kings of the Egyptians, to come upon us.
>
> Wherefore they arose [the Syrian army] and fled in the twilight, and left their tents, and their horses, and their asses, even the camp as it was, and fled for their life. (2 Kings 7:6–7)

Just after this, the lepers arrived to find the spoils the Syrians had left: food still over the fire and clothing and supplies in abundance. It was just as the prophet Elisha had said it would be. Because of their decision to take action instead of sit and wait, these four were the first to rejoice in the surplus. (See 2 Kings 7:8–16.)

Emerson beautifully explains how our capacities grow and how our tasks become easier, *"That which we try to do, and persist in doing, becomes easy to do, not because its nature is changed, but because our power to do is developed."*[6] There will be many times on your mission when you are faced with the decision to take action and go the extra mile. It is during those times when you will be required to dig deep and find the strength within yourself and within the power of the Atonement. The times we decide to rise to the challenge during those "extra mile hours" benefit us as we deepen our foundation for the eternities to come. There are many great principles taught to us by the Savior in the parable of the wise man who built his house upon the rock. Luke quoted Christ as saying, "He is like a man which built an house, *and digged deep*, and laid the foundation on a rock: and when the flood arose, the stream beat vehemently upon that house, and could not shake it: for it was founded upon a rock" (Luke 6:48; emphasis added). The Savior tells us that the wise man "digged deep." There is great meaning in that thought. When we dig deep to lay our foundation, when adversity comes, we are safe and unshakeable.

Years ago, the tallest two buildings in the world were built and finished in 1998 in Malaysia. These buildings were called the Petronas Towers. For six years, these buildings were the tallest in the world

Diligence Is Key

125

until the taller Taipei 101 was finished in 2004 in Thailand. In the past ten years, there have been other buildings built that surpass all of these structures in height. The Petronas Towers stand 1,483 feet tall, and they are a remarkable architectural feat.[7] There is something even greater than the height of the buildings that most people don't know about these towers. The Petronas Towers are no longer the world's tallest buildings, but they still carry the title of having the "deepest seated foundation" of any building in the world.[8] When they first started construction on the Petronas Towers, it was discovered that the original site was only supported by half limestone and half bedrock. A critical engineering decision was made to move the entire site two hundred meters so the building could rest completely upon bedrock. The bedrock beneath the Petronas Towers is extraordinarily deep. To reach safe and secure bedrock to support these two magnificent structures, 104 concrete piles were poured from 197 to 300 feet deep. Structurally, there is no building in the world with a deeper and stronger foundation.[9]

How does a missionary establish a foundation deep enough and strong enough to carry the title of the "most deep seated foundation?" You must be willing to dig deep. Digging deep is not just doing what every other missionary does or just doing enough to get by. Digging deep is not just opening your mouth when it is easy or just obeying the easy rules. Digging deep requires more effort, more persistence, more spirit, more heart, and more desire than just normal digging.

Here are a few thoughts about how a full-time missionary "digging deep" in their missionary labors parallels the building of a great structure or the building of a great mission.

1. It is not easy to reach critical depth when building; it cannot be casually approached.
2. It takes careful planning, research, and study to build on a correct and firm foundation.
3. It takes diligent work and proper tools.
4. It is about searching until you find the bedrock (Christ and His principles).
5. The foundation must be properly dug before the storm or adversity comes.

6. Christ must be your architect, foundation, and cornerstone.

7. With Christ as your foundation, your house "cannot be shaken." (See Luke 6:48.)

When I think of digging deep, I see a missionary who is sweating after a hard day's work. I see an elder or sister who never lets rain or sleet affect their service. I see a missionary who is faithfully studying their scriptures, language, and assigned readings each day. (This is not superficial skimming of the word of God; rather it is earnest, prayerful reading and pondering.) I see a missionary who is desperately trying to listen to the Spirit in all things. I see a missionary on their knees fervently pleading to have the Spirit of God as they teach. I see a missionary who only has a little seedling of a testimony when he enters the MTC, but through patience, diligence, and faith, transforms that seedling into a mighty oak by the end of his mission. I see a missionary founded on the principles of obedience working through being with a tough companion or the frequent temptation to break mission rules. I see a missionary who follows Christ in every footstep. I see a young man or young woman who has learned he or she is merely an instrument in the hands of the mighty Savior. When I think of digging deep, I think of a powerful stripling warrior who is without fear as he testifies boldly of the Savior Jesus Christ. These missionaries cannot be swayed from the faith because their foundation is so deep.

When times are hard and your mission stretches your limits, go the extra mile, take action, and dig deep to establish your foundation. I invite you to elevate your efforts a little more in the service of our God as you "go with him twain" (Matthew 5:41).

Your friend,
Brother Jeff Erickson

Diligence Is Key

NOTES

1.   Gordon B. Hinckley, "The Quest for Excellence," *BYU Speeches*, November 1998.

2.   James E. Faust, "I Believe I Can, I Knew I Could," *Ensign*, November 2003.

3.   Ibid.

4.   Peter Vidmar, "Pursuing Excellence," *Ensign*, May 1985; David G. Savage, "Interviews With 120 Artists, Athletes and Scholars: The Key to Success? It's Drive, Not Talent, Study Finds," *Los Angeles Times*, February 17, 1985, articles. latimes.com/1985-02-17/news/mn-3575_1_top-artists.

5.   Vidmar, "Pursuing Excellence."

6.   Timothy Titcomb [Josiah Gilbert Holland], *Gold-Foil: Hammered from Popular Proverbs* (New York: Charles Scribner, 1859), 291; emphasis added.

7.   *Wikipedia*, s.v. "Taipei 101," last modified February 21, 2017, en.wikipedia. org/wiki/Taipei_101.

8.   "Foundation System of PETRONAS Tower," *Foundation, Concrete and Earthquake Engineering*, accessed February 22, 2017, civil-engg-world.blogspot. com/2013/02/Foundation-system-PETRONAS-Tower.html.

9.   *Wikipedia*, s.v. "Petronas Towers," last modified February 10, 2017, en.wikipedia.org/wiki/Petronas_Towers.

Diligence Is Key

"LET US LABOR DILIGENTLY"

Dear Elders and Sisters,

I remember a story about President Hinckley writing a letter to his father when he was on his mission. He was facing no success in his missionary endeavors. He said, "I am wasting my time and your money. I don't see any point in my staying here." A loving but strong reply came from his father. That letter read: "Dear Gordon. I have your letter. . . . I have only one suggestion. Forget yourself and go to work, With love, Your Father."[1] The message of those words has always rung true to me. When we are discouraged, we simply need to go to work and do more of the right things.

Mormon gives this powerful admonition to his son in the difficult times in which they lived: "And now, my beloved son, notwithstanding their hardness, let us labor diligently; for if we should cease to labor, we should be brought under condemnation; for we have a labor to perform whilst in this tabernacle of clay, that we may conquer the enemy of all righteousness, and rest our souls in the kingdom of God" (Moroni 9:6). I love his powerful directive, "let us labor diligently." I have observed numerous missionaries in my life. I can say without hesitation that those who labor diligently enjoy their missions, have sacred experiences, and return home full of faith and confidence that they have served the Lord well. Those who spend many hours in idleness do not have the same peace, and experience more regret in regards to their mission. Jacob said, "And how blessed are they who have labored diligently in his vineyard" (Jacob 6:3). I testify that Jacob's statement is true; when we diligently serve the Lord, He pours out his richest blessings upon us.

Brother Jack Christianson, a CES instructor, shared this experience, which occurred when President Hinckley was the prophet. President Monson received a package in the mail containing two pairs of roller blades and a little note. "The note said, 'President Monson, one pair is for you, one pair is for President Faust so you can try to keep up with President Hinckley.' "[2] President Hinckley was a prophet and a servant who always labored diligently.

Today, the call is the same as it was in Book of Mormon times. "Wherefore we labored diligently among our people, that we might persuade them to come unto Christ, and partake of the goodness of God, that they might enter into his rest" (Jacob 1:7). As missionaries, the best recipe for persuading others to come unto Christ is diligent labor. There is a Greek proverb that says, "He that will have the fruit, must climb the tree." Missionary work is certainly about sharing the fruit, partaking of the fruit, and enjoying the fruits of our labors.

The Lord said in our day, "Let every man be diligent in all things. And the idler shall not have place in the church, except he repent and mend his ways" (D&C 75:29). For the missionaries not laboring diligently, it is time to repent. Samuel the Lamanite said this of his faithful people, "They are striving with unwearied diligence that they may bring the remainder of their brethren to the knowledge of the truth" (Helaman 15:6). May we be as the Lamanites, demonstrating "unwearied diligence" (Helaman 15:6), and may we "receive the reward of the laborer" (D&C 23:7) in our missionary labors.

As a father, I have tried to instill in my children the desire to work. Sometimes I have been successful and other times not as much. One Saturday, when I was attempting to motivate my son Taft to do his jobs, he was standing around more than he was working. He was reflecting on the difficulties of his family stewardship when he said, "When I get older, I am going to have a butler." There is not a missionary in the world that needs a butler or a maid; rather, they all need to work like a faithful butler or maid.

One of my favorite commissions in the Book of Mormon is found in the book of Ether. The brother of Jared and his people had been on the beach for four years and had been pretty comfortable. The Lord came to the brother of Jared and said, "Go to work and build" (Ether 2:16). He was referring to the building of barges, but the phrase can apply to so many aspects of our missions and our lives. Go to work and build a better ward, branch, or area. Go to work and build a successful life through repentance and embracing the gospel. Go to work and build a successful teaching pool. Go to work and build a successful missionary-minded ward. Go to work, and invite everyone to come unto Christ and be saved. There is something powerful about "going to work."

I once heard a story told of a young man who was called into his father's den. Once there, his father says, "I need to borrow one hundred dollars of your money. I would like you to go and earn one hundred dollars for me."

The son said, "Okay."

He went to his mother and told her the deal with Dad, and so she said, "Oh, here is one hundred dollars. You go and have fun."

For the next week, he had fun as he played and relaxed. At the end of the week, he went to his father in the den and gave him the one hundred dollars his mother had given him. His father took the money and threw it into the fire.

The son looked at his dad like he was crazy and asked, "What are you doing?"

Both father and son watched as the bills burned.

The father said, "That was not the one hundred dollars I was looking for." The father said again to the son, "I would like you to go earn one hundred dollars and I would like to borrow it."

"Okay," said the son.

This time he went to his grandmother, who really wanted to spend some time with him. He told her of the deal with his father. This time, she gave him one hundred dollars so they could spend the week together having fun. At the end of the week, he went to his father again and gave him the one hundred dollars. The father again looked at the money and threw it in the fire.

The son again looked at his dad and asked, "What are you doing?"

To which the father replied, "That is not the one hundred dollars that I need." They watched the bills burn again. This time, the dad made the same agreement with his son. "I need you to earn one hundred dollars, and then I would like to borrow it from you."

This time, the son went out and earned the one hundred dollars. He cut lawns, pulled weeds, hedged yards, trimmed bushes, cleared brush, and worked very hard all week. By the end of the week, his muscles were sore, his body was exhausted, but he had the one hundred dollars.

He went to his father in the den. He handed his father the one hundred dollars, and his father again took the bills, looked at them, and threw them in the fire. This time, the boy thrust his hand into the fire and retrieved the bills and brushed them off. The father turned to his son, and said, "That is the one hundred dollars I have been looking for."

A mission is like the story of the one hundred dollars. When you serve the Lord faithfully and labor diligently, you wouldn't trade that time for anything in the world. You would sacrifice everything because that work is of such great worth to you. President Ezra Taft Benson said, "One of the greatest secrets of missionary work is work! If a missionary works, he will get the Spirit; if he gets the Spirit, he will teach by the Spirit; and if he teaches by the Spirit, he will touch the hearts of the people and he will be happy. There will be no homesickness, no worrying about families, for [he will have] all [his] time and talents and interests . . . centered on the work of the ministry. Work, work, work— there is no satisfactory substitute, especially in missionary work."[3]

I pray that you will go out and labor diligently for the rest of your mission. May it be said of you as was said of Alma, Ammon, and his brethren, "Behold, they have labored exceedingly" (Alma 29:15).

Your friend,
Brother Jeff Erickson

NOTES

1.   Jeffrey R. Holland, "President Gordon B. Hinckley: Stalwart and Brave He Stands," *Ensign*, June 1995.

2.   Jack R. Christianson, *It Takes Faith* (Covenant Communications, 2002), audio CD.

3.   Ezra Taft Benson, *The Teachings of Ezra Taft Benson* (Salt Lake City: Bookcraft, 1988), 200.

Diligence Is Key

SHORTCUTS

Dear Elders and Sisters,

I recently got a message from a man whose son was coming to interview me about business and career choices. He was at BYU trying to determine his major and future career, and he wanted to talk to me about life's critical principles. Before the visit, his father texted me and said, "When you meet with him, talk to him about the importance of education and good grades." I know that what he was really saying was, "Tell him there are no shortcuts to success; first, you must pay the price."

As a missionary, an important principle to realize is that with the Lord, there are no shortcuts. Heavenly Father has young men serve for twenty-four months and young women serve for eighteen months for specific reasons. We complete our missions faithfully because that is what the Lord has asked us to do, and He has a plan for our lives. We trust in Him and do things His way because His ways are higher than our ways, and His way always works. (See Isaiah 55:9.)

There are people out there who don't want to study, but still want to get good grades. There are people who are not willing to work hard, but who still want to be rich in terms of the world's standards. There are people who are willing to receive, but who don't want to give. Life's most precious gifts require effort, not idleness. The law of the harvest still remains as one of the wonderful laws of the Lord.

In a powerful conference talk, Richard L. Evans taught, "Many years ago Emerson wrote an essay, 'Compensation,' in which he said: . . . 'it is impossible to get anything without its price.' . . . I heard from President Lee a very short sentence that said essentially what

Emerson said, that there are no successful sinners. It is a remarkable sentence to contemplate."[1]

I love this story told by Elder Dallin H. Oaks:

> Two other powerful ideas were given voice by a noble young woman who survived a terrible experience. Virginia Reed was a survivor of the tragic Donner-Reed party, who made one of the earliest wagon treks into California. If this wagon train had followed the established Oregon Trail from Fort Bridger (Wyoming) northwest to Fort Hall (Idaho) and then southwest toward California, they would have reached their destination in safety. Instead, they were misled by a promoter. Lansford W. Hastings persuaded them they could save significant distance and time by following his so-called Hastings Cutoff. The Donner-Reed party left the proven trail at Fort Bridger and struggled southwest. They blazed a trail through the rugged Wasatch Mountains and then south of the Great Salt Lake and westward over the soggy surface of the salt flats in furnace heat.
>
> The delays and incredible energies expended on this unproven route cost the Donner-Reed party an extra month in reaching the Sierra Nevada Mountains. As they hastened up the eastern slope trying to beat the first snows, they were caught in a tragic winter storm only one day short of the summit and a downhill passage into California. Marooned for the winter, half their group perished from starvation and cold.
>
> After months in the mountains and incredible hardships of hunger and terror, thirteen-year-old Virginia Reed reached California and sent a letter to her cousin in the Midwest. After recounting her experiences and the terrible sufferings of their party, she concluded with this wise advice: "Never take no cutoffs [sic] and hury [sic] along as fast as you can."[2]

In life, "cutoffs" and shortcuts don't work in the plan of salvation. The Lord has a plan for us, and we need to participate in and embrace our role in that plan. We need to use our agency to become what He would have us become. It won't happen overnight, but it will happen as Alma said.

> But if ye will nourish the word, yea, nourish the tree as it beginneth to grow, by your faith with great diligence, and with patience, looking forward to the fruit thereof, it shall take root; and behold it shall be a tree springing up unto everlasting life.

Diligence Is Key

And because of your diligence and your faith and your patience with the word in nourishing it, that it may take root in you, behold, by and by ye shall pluck the fruit thereof, which is most precious, which is sweet above all that is sweet, and which is white above all that is white, yea, and pure above all that is pure; and ye shall feast upon this fruit even until ye are filled, that ye hunger not, neither shall ye thirst. (Alma 32:41–42)

Two years ago, a young woman's family came to the commencement ceremonies at Quinnipiac University in Connecticut. They were excited to watch their daughter graduate after four years of college studies. The problem was that, unknown to them, their daughter had attempted to take a shortcut in her life. She had taken the thousands of dollars her family had sent her for school and spent it. She had dropped out of college and now her day of reckoning had arrived. The daughter showed up on graduation day in a cap and gown, in order to continue the dishonest charade, but the lie began to unravel when her mother couldn't get a ticket to the ramp where graduate pictures were being taken. Her mother called to ask why, and she was told that her daughter was not even enrolled. Her name was not on the program. At one point, the daughter panicked, and, hoping to avert the outcome, actually called in a bomb threat so the commencement exercises would not proceed. In the end, the ruse was discovered and the non-student was not only humiliated, but also arrested and imprisoned.[3]

A mission can be very similar for some missionaries whose wonderful parents send a young son or daughter into the mission field and assume that he or she is being schooled by the Lord. In most instances, this occurs and the educational experience is inspired and remarkable. In a few instances, however, young missionaries like this student will physically, spiritually, mentally, and emotionally drop out of their mission experience. They believe they can shortcut their mission and still receive the same blessings, benefits, and educational benefits. They are supported financially, but they do not do their part as an emissary of Christ. The Lord, in His infinite wisdom, does not reward shortcuts; there is no reward for a missionary who does not labor, love, serve, teach, and testify. An elder or sister who has not paid the price will not qualify for attributes and traits that are patiently learned through hard work, application, and perseverance.

Diligence Is Key

135

There are no shortcuts to the kingdom of God, so enjoy the journey and make sure you travel with faith, diligence, and patience. Here is a wonderful promise to remember as you travel on the Lord's path:

> And I will also be your light in the wilderness; and I will prepare the way before you, if it so be that ye shall keep my commandments; wherefore, inasmuch as ye shall keep my commandments ye shall be led towards the promised land; and ye shall know that it is by me that ye are led.
>
> Yea, and the Lord said also that: After ye have arrived in the promised land, ye shall know that I, the Lord, am God; and that I, the Lord, did deliver you from destruction. (1 Nephi 17:13–14)

Your friend,
Brother Jeff Erickson

Diligence Is Key

NOTES

1. Richard L. Evans, "Should the Commandments Be Rewritten?," *Ensign*, November 1971.
2. Dallin H. Oaks, "Powerful Ideas," *Ensign*, November 1995.
3. Michael Melia, "Police arrest women in Quinnipiac bomb threats," *Boston Globe*, May 19, 2014.

TIME

Dear Elders and Sisters,

A few years ago, my daughter, Holland, reminded me of a valuable principle with some simple words. She and I were spending time together cleaning up some things around the house, when she found a watch. She put the watch on her wrist and then called out to me. She said, "Dad, we don't have much time." In those simple words, she spoke such a profound truth. For missionaries, there truly isn't much time.

As a missionary, you have been learning about the principle of time and time management. The amazing thing about a mission is that while there are some long days, the two years or eighteen months of a mission go by so fast. In my life, I have learned that time is not only precious, but it is also priceless. We all have only been allotted so much time. I was a bishop for five-and-a-half years, and it felt like it was only two years. The experiences were amazing, but I've always wished that I would have had more time as a bishop. There were some things I would have loved to have done and loved to have taught, and some others things I would have loved for the ward to accomplish under my stewardship as bishop. Likewise, I am certain that every missionary wishes he could have a little time from his mission back.

My plea to you is to use your time wisely. Make the most of your mission experience. Now is the time for you to serve with all your heart, might, mind, and strength. There is no better time to be called a servant of Jesus Christ. The devoted time you spend now will never be regretted later if you are faithful in your service. This is the time to be a faithful elder or sister for The Church of Jesus Christ of Latter-day Saints.

Diligence Is Key

There is great depth in the words of the second verse of the hymn, "Improve the Shining Moments." It reads,

Time flies on wings of lightning
We cannot call it back.
It comes, then passes forward
Along its onward track.
And if we are not mindful,
The chance will fade away,
For life is quick in passing.
'Tis as a single day.[1]

Time is full of wonderful blessings. The most precious moments of time on your mission will be your most treasured.

Benjamin Franklin said, "Dost thou love Life? Then do not squander Time; for that's the Stuff Life is made of."[2] He also said, "Lost time is never found again" (Ibid.). Samuel Smiles said, "Lost wealth may be replaced by industry, lost knowledge by study, lost health by temperance or medicine, but lost time is gone forever."[3]

A mission is the greatest training ground for the effectively using your time. You are taught to plan and organize your days. You are taught to not waste time, but to be efficient in your plan. You are taught to use time to take care of your physical and spiritual health. You are taught to use time to bring others to the kingdom of God. The greatest balance of your time in your life will probably be as a missionary. Why does the Lord teach us to manage our time as missionaries? Because, for the rest of your earthly sojourn, you will need to be an effective user of the time He has allotted you.

As a father, my time is juggled between my own physical and spiritual strengthening and being a husband, father, and provider. These areas all could require the bulk of our time, but a loving Heavenly Father says, "Establish . . . a house of order" (D&C 88:119). We must then place priorities upon our allotted time. The number one priority, in my opinion, is personal spirituality and righteousness. If we are not taking time to strengthen our lives spiritually, we will not be able to elevate others.

Years ago, President Kimball shared this story years from an unknown author:

Diligence Is Key

And in my dreams I came to a beautiful building, somehow like a bank, and yet not a bank because the brass marker said, "Time for Sale."

I saw a man, breathless and pale; painfully pull himself up the stairs like a sick man. I heard him say: "The doctor told me I was five years too late in going to see him. I will buy those five years now—and then he can save my life."

Then came another man; also who said to the clerk: "When it was too late, I discovered that God had given me great capacities and endowments, and I failed to develop them. Sell me ten years so that I can be the man I would have been."

Then came a younger man to say: "The company has told me that starting next month I can have a big job if I am prepared to take it. But I am not prepared. Give me two years of time so that I will be prepared to take the job next month."

So they came, ill, hopeless, despondent, worried, unhappy—and they left smiling, each man with a look of unutterable pleasure on his face, for he had what he so desperately needed and wanted—time.

Then I awakened, glad that I had what these men had not, and what they could never buy—time. Time to do so many things I wanted to do, that I must do. If that morning I whistled at my work, it was because a great happiness filled my heart. For I still had time, *if* I used it well.[4]

May your time as a missionary be precious. May you learn the things that a wise Heavenly Father would have you learn during this two-year or eighteen-month time period. May you use your time wisely because it is limited. May you realize that time is a stewardship. May you leave your mission grateful for the time you had to serve the Lord and teach His principles.

A few years ago, I knew a young father who was married with three kids and who began having headaches. He finally went to the doctor and was, in turn, sent to a specialist. The specialist advised him that he had only about three months to live. I know that must have been a bitter pill for him and his family to swallow. He had a wonderful wife who essentially said, "Let's make the most of that time. I would love for you to make videos for the kids, write down precious things, and record what you want them to remember about you." She was encouraging and understanding, but was also trying to work through the difficulties that lay ahead.

Diligence Is Key

Unfortunately, her husband had been spending his free time for the last several years playing video games. He was so addicted to this routine that rather than spend his final days with his wife and children—recording precious writings, giving pieces of advice and direction, and doing things of great worth—he spent his last weeks playing video games. In the last weeks of his life, and with little time left, he chose gaming over family.

May you learn to spend your time as missionaries doing the most precious and important things you can do with the little time you have. May you learn during your mission to love, teach, inspire, obey, testify, invite, challenge, serve, honor, build, pray, and lead. May you learn to be led by the Spirit, be bold, be an instrument, have great faith, be courageous, be grateful, use the priesthood, call down the powers of heaven, see the goodness of God, and cherish the Atonement of Jesus Christ. If you do these things with your time, the Lord will say, "Well done [my] good and faithful servant" (Matthew 25:21). May you treasure your time as a servant of Jesus Christ.

Your friend,
Brother Jeff Erickson

NOTES

1. Improve the Shining Moments, *Hymns*, 226.
2. Benjamin Franklin, *Poor Richard's Almanack* (The Peter Pauper Press, 1981).
3. Tryon Edwards, *A Dictionary of Thoughts* (Detroit: F. B. Dickerson, 1908), 577.
4. Spencer W. Kimball, "Planning for a Full and Abundant Life," *Ensign*, May 1974; emphasis in original.

WAKE UP

Dear Elders and Sisters,

Not too long ago, my six-year-old daughter, Holland, was shopping with her grandma for school clothes. Holland was on a mission to go to a handful of stores and find some specific things. The time they had was winding down, and Holland knew they had to leave the mall soon. Holland felt like her grandma was not moving fast enough. As Holland hurried to another store, she turned to her grandma and said, "Come on Grandma, we have to pick up the pace."

A few years back, I was an elders quorum president in my ward. A member of the elders quorum presidency and I were out two nights a week ministering to members of the ward. Many blessings came as we saw people come back to church, helped less-active priests receive the Melchizedek priesthood, and saw other members baptized. These visits were edifying, spiritually rewarding, and very personally satisfying. As a presidency, we felt great about our efforts, and I felt good about the Lord's blessings of success in our labors. During this time, I had a wonderful stake president who had the vision of what we should be doing as an elders quorum presidency. He would have every elders quorum president and high priests group leader in the stake come to a meeting once a month to review our ministering efforts and Melchizedek priesthood efforts. At one of those meetings, I had a great wake-up call.

The stake president was talking about living what we teach. At one point, in one of these meetings, he had everyone put their heads down and close their eyes. He then said, "Everyone who is reading their scriptures every day, and having a kneeling prayer twice a day raise your hand." Now, I didn't cheat by looking, so I have no idea how many hands went up in the air, but I know that I wasn't as faithful as

I should have been in those two important spiritual areas. I remember desperately wanting to raise my hand so the stake president wouldn't think less of me and so that I wouldn't disappoint him, but I was not faithful in living some of those vital, yet simple commandments. I was praying, but not with the earnestness and the daily devotion that I should have been praying with, and I was not always kneeling. I was reading my scriptures casually, but not every day.

This meeting pierced my soul and was one of those times where the Spirit said, "Jeff, you are not doing what you should be, and you are not nearly as spiritually great as you think you are. You need to repent and change." I hated that I couldn't raise my hand, and I hated that I wasn't true and faithful in a few precious areas. Once my feelings of personal disappointment left me, I was grateful for the awakening from a servant of God. I repented and improved and was thankful that the Lord's servant woke me from my spiritual slumber. I haven't been perfect since that event, but I have been much improved. I have even had streaks of time where I have not missed for months or years in my prayers and scripture study.

I felt that the Lord was telling me what Lehi told his children, "Awake, my sons; put on the armor of righteousness. Shake off the chains with which ye are bound, and come forth out of obscurity, and arise from the dust" (2 Nephi 1:23). I wanted to do better and be more righteous. I left that meeting knowing that I needed to increase my level of personal righteousness.

Nephi said, "Awake, my soul! No longer droop in sin. Rejoice, O my heart, and give place no more for the enemy of my soul" (2 Nephi 4:28). I am saying the same thing to you as missionaries. If you are asleep in your missionary calling, if you are underperforming, if you are disobedient, or if you are lazy, now is the time to awake. I recently attended a missionary homecoming, and the missionary reminded the audience that you have two years to serve a mission and the rest of your life to think about it. He said that, in the last four days since he returned home, he had been reflecting on that statement repeatedly.

Jacob emphasizes this principle when he says, "Awake, awake! Put on strength, O arm of the Lord; awake as in the ancient days" (2 Nephi 8:9). The only way to recover and gain strength as a missionary is to wake up and serve with all your heart, mind, and strength. Alma said to the righteous in Gideon, "And now my beloved brethren, I have said these things unto you that I might awaken you to a sense of your duty to God, that ye may walk blameless before him, that ye may walk after the holy order of God, after which ye have been received" (Alma 7:22). These words were spoken to good members of the Church that needed to multiply their efforts, increase their speed, lengthen their stride, and expand their level of obedience and faithfulness.

J. M. Power said, "If you want to make your dreams come true, the first thing you have to do is wake up."[1] Another great quote with powerful missionary application is, "Wake up with determination, go to bed with satisfaction."[2] For every missionary not serving as they should, Paul's simple words should suffice, "Awake to righteousness, and sin not" (1 Corinthians 15:34). Paul also said, "And that, knowing the time, that now it is high time to awake out of sleep" (Romans 13:11). I would exhort every missionary who is performing below their potential to realize it is "high time" to wake up, repent, and start over by serving with more vigor and vitality.

As a bishop, there were many times when someone would come into my office with problems. Most of the time, these problems resulted from sin. As we would discuss the issues, one of the principles that the Lord would teach the individual and myself was that they needed to awake, arise, and get going on a pathway of repentance and righteousness. They needed to move away from poor decisions and poor choices, leaving behind the bondage and snare of sin, in order to step onto the strait and narrow path. Jacob said, "O my brethren, hearken unto my words; arouse the faculties of your souls; shake yourselves that ye may awake from the slumber of death; and loose yourselves from the pains of hell that ye may not become angels to the devil, to be cast into that lake of fire and brimstone which is the second death" (Jacob 3:11).

As a bishop, I often witnessed the truth of Jacob's words and was always grateful when people awoke from their spiritual slumber, moving forward with righteous decisions and repentance. It is important to know that no matter how deep your slumber or sleep is, the Lord will help you wake up. Alma said, "Behold, he changed their hearts; yea, he awakened them out of a deep sleep, and they awoke unto God" (Alma 5:7). May every missionary who is idle, inactive, disobedient, and asleep at his post wake up unto God.

Years ago, I heard a story of a man who had a powerful habit in his life. I have not been able to verify the story, whether fact or fiction, but the principle it taught is powerful. The man would have his servant come in and wake him early each morning and say, "Wake up! Wake up! You've got great things to accomplish today." I have to believe that every full-time servant of Christ should do the same. Wouldn't it be great if your companion woke you early each day and said, "Wake up! Wake up! You've got great things to accomplish today"? The Lord said, "Awake, O kings [and queens] of the earth! Come ye, O, come ye, with your gold and your silver, to the help of my people" (D&C 124:11). As missionaries, you are destined to be kings and queens, leaders and helpers bringing people to truth and light. May you fulfill that sacred destiny as you wake-up, pick up your pace, and serve faithfully.

Your friend,
Brother Jeff Erickson

NOTES

1. Cindy Trimm, *Push: Persevere until Success Happens through Prayer* (Destiny Image, 2014).
2. Anonymous in Richard Shivers, *The Happy Christian: Pearls of Christian Wisdom* (Lulu Press, 2016).

A GOD OF MERCY

Dear Elders and Sisters,

I remember a priceless moment between my young sons Tanner and Tyler. One night, Tanner wouldn't eat his soup. I was trying to get him to eat better, so I made him stay at the table and eat. This process took a long time. Tanner sat at the table crying and wailing because he did not want to eat the soup, but I was showing no mercy. Tyler came into the kitchen, evaluated the situation, and said, "Dad, I'll just eat it for him and then he can go to bed." It was a great act of mercy by an older brother with a heart full of kindness.

I have studied the gospel for years now, and I continue to learn new principles and doctrines all the time. My favorite principle, and one that I learn over and over again, is that the God of the Mormons, the God of Israel, the God of the New Testament, the God of the Doctrine and Covenants, the God of the Book of Mormon, and the God of the living prophets is an absolutely merciful God. The God I believe in is a God of unlimited mercy. God is quick to forgive, rescue, succor, heal, comfort, and reassure. The God we study about and pray to is full of "abundant mercy" (Alma 18:41). It is no wonder that Alma called God's plan "the plan of mercy" (Alma 42:15).

I can testify of this merciful God because I have felt in my life the "pure mercies of God" (Moroni 8:19) and "the multitude of his tender mercies" (1 Nephi 8:8). I have witnessed His hand as it has touched my life and the lives of others over and over again. There are few occasions in life that are sweeter and more powerful than when the "arms of mercy" are extended to us in our trying moments (Mosiah 16:12).

A few years ago, I was very upset with my son Tanner. I don't even remember what he did, but I was at the end of my rope. I was so mad that I chased him around the house and into his room. As he ran into his room, with me close behind, he said, "Have mercy, have mercy." Those profound words immediately softened my heart, and mercy was granted and no discipline was administered.

As missionaries, your greatest objective is to invite people to feel the mercy and love of God. You testify to them that you know how they can feel lifted, strengthened, and sustained, if they will apply your message. I cannot think of anything better to testify of than the message that there is a merciful God who will encircle them in the arms of His love.

I saw a simple, precious example of this pure love one day with my four-year-old son Taft and baby daughter, Holland. She was screaming and crying. Little Taft didn't know what to do, but he so badly wanted to console his precious little sister he loved so much. He took her and held her in his arms and rocked her and said, "Don't cry, it's okay. You are still pretty."

I have felt the arms and the love of a merciful Father comfort and console me. When I feel His love, I am calmed and assured that all will be well and that the storm will pass. I can easily picture a loving Heavenly Father comforting and lifting His missionaries when they need support in their most difficult moments. I can see our all-loving, all-merciful Father sweeping you up in His arms and saying, "Don't worry my son (or daughter), everything will be okay. I am with you. I will be your guide. Take my yoke upon you. You are my child, and I love you. I will never leave you comfortless. You are priceless to me."

I believe God shows us mercy in our lives in many simple ways. Many years ago, our family was at Disney World. We were exploring the area around the resort we were staying in. We came to a pathway bordered with poles on either side—six to eighteen inches high. They ran for about 150 feet. My sons began to climb on these poles and attempted to walk the entire 150-foot path on top of the poles. I remember saying I would offer each of them one dollar if they could make it the whole way without falling off. Tyler and Tanner, the older boys, accomplished the feat, but little two-and-a-half-year-old Blake couldn't do it. He kept falling off. He was getting more and more frustrated because he kept falling off every few feet. Finally, I said, "Blake, let me help." This time, Blake climbed on top of the poles and began to walk as I gently held his hand. This simple assistance made it possible for Blake to succeed. There were a few times when he lost his balance, and I offered much firmer assistance. With this extra help, Blake eventually walked across all of the poles and reached the end of the path. He was excited about his accomplishment and appreciated the extra help.

I believe Heavenly Father operates in a similar fashion. As we walk the pathway of righteousness, we can't do it alone. We need the power of His help. His tender mercies along the way help us stay on track. Occasionally, we need even more strength and support to continue the difficult journey. The arm, or hand of God, which is His power, keeps us moving forward toward our celestial destination. This is all done for us because of the mercy of a loving Father who would do anything appropriate and righteous to help us return home.

Here are a few powerful scriptural principles and blessings of God's mercy that are vital to remember:

"And thus doth the Lord work with his power in all cases among the children of men, extending the arm of mercy towards them that put their trust in him" (Mosiah 29:20).

"For the Lord hath comforted his people, and will have mercy upon his afflicted" (1 Nephi 21:16).

"And thus mercy can satisfy the demands of justice, and encircles them in the arms of safety" (Alma 34:16).

"But blessed are they who have kept the covenant and observed the commandment, for they shall obtain mercy" (D&C 54:6).

"For I, the Lord, show mercy unto all the meek" (D&C 97:2).

"Whosoever repenteth shall find mercy" (Alma 32:13).

"And mercy claimeth the penitent, and mercy cometh because of the atonement" (Alma 42:23).

"Behold, mine arm of mercy is extended towards you, and whosoever will come, him will I receive; and blessed are those who come unto me" (3 Nephi 9:14).

Dearest missionaries, be meek, repent, trust in Him, and come unto Him. Because of the wonderful Atonement of Christ, you will be encircled in the arms of safety—His mercy. Elder Holland said this about God's mercy: "It underscores the thought I heard many years ago that surely the thing that God enjoys most about being God is the thrill of being merciful, especially to those who don't expect it and often feel they don't deserve it."[1]

One final act of mercy that I must mention occurred on the day my son Tyler returned from his mission. Our family went out to eat to celebrate Tyler's return. After dinner, we each grabbed a circular mint candy as we left the restaurant and walked along the sidewalk of the strip mall. We were in a store when our little Holland, age six, got the mint lodged in her throat and was suddenly choking and couldn't breathe. A moment that had been so joyous was turning quickly into one of terror. Holland was unable to free the candy on her own. We acted quickly and did the Heimlich maneuver on her. On the second or third attempt, the obstructed candy was expelled. Holland began to cry, and I don't know that I have ever heard such a wonderful sound in all my life. I went home that day one of the most grateful fathers in the world, for a lifetime of heartache and sorrow was taken away in an absolutely merciful moment.

I testify that there is a God of mercy who is quick to guide, lift, and sustain His children. I testify that we believe in a God whose "bowels are filled with mercy" (3 Nephi 17:7). I would invite you to remember the words of Amulek, who said, "Yea, cry unto him for mercy; for he is mighty to save" (Alma 34:18). May you plead as so many in the scriptures have, "O God have mercy on me," (For example, see Psalms 9:13, 51:1.) and I promise you will feel a multitude of His tender mercies.

Your friend,
Brother Jeff Erickson

NOTES

1. Jeffrey R. Holland "The Laborers in the Vineyard," *Ensign*, May 2012.

GOD IS WITH YOU

Dear Elders and Sisters,

I had a powerful experience, a few years ago, before the construction of the Gilbert Arizona Temple commenced. We had a gathering of the youth in our stake in celebration of the new temple being built. There were many youth leaders there, and part of the experience was for the youth to walk to the temple grounds along a path that was lined by many leaders. We were to be quiet as the youth walked toward the temple grounds. As I observed the youth participate in this experience, the Spirit taught me something. Most of the youth walked by me in groups of varying sizes, but occasionally there was a young man or young woman walking alone. As I observed one young man in particular walking alone, the Spirit said to me, "This is one of the vital reasons for the temple, so that you will never be alone." This powerful truth left a deep impression on me. I am so grateful that a merciful Heavenly Father does not want us to be lonely. I believe the same is true for you on your mission. As you are sharing a message of unity, family, companionship, and Christ, God wants you to feel His presence, reassurance, companionship, and love.

I believe all of us have tasted and felt loneliness. Most missionaries will experience times of loneliness when things are tough and companionship relationships are taxed. Loneliness is a powerful feeling, and its effects can be a master teacher in our lives. In the moments when we are the most alone, we may also be the most aware of the One who is always there. As a missionary, you must remember that you are not ever really alone. You have the greatest companion there is—the Lord, Jesus Christ who is always by your side. One of His great promises to missionaries is, "And whoso receiveth you, there I will be also, for I will go before your face. I will be on your right hand and on your left, and my Spirit shall be in your hearts, and mine angels round about you, to bear you up" (D&C 84:88). In times when you feel alone, afraid, or abandoned, I pray that you will remember this verse: "Behold, the kingdom is yours. And behold, and lo, I am with the faithful always. Even so. Amen" (D&C 62:9). This heart-warming promise can carry you during those periods of loneliness as a missionary. The Lord will be there for you to lift, comfort, bless, reassure, succor, and speak peace to your soul.

One of my seminary teachers in high school was Brother Bassett. He was a terrific teacher, and I developed a great relationship with him. A few years ago, he shared this story about a young man in his ward from Mona, Utah, named Johnny. This young man's brother died at age nineteen, a few years before Johnny went on his mission. Shortly after, Johnny served a worthy mission and returned home. Brother Bassett spoke to him after he returned and asked, "Did you ever have an experience on your mission where you felt like your brother was there with you?" Johnny said, "I never felt my brother's presence until I had a powerful experience when my companion and I were tracting one day. We knocked on a door and a lady answered and told us she wasn't interested. We were thirsty and asked her if we might have a glass of water, so she retrieved the water and came back out to the doorstep. When she returned, she was carrying three glasses of water. She came out, and said, 'Where is the other guy?' My companion and I assured her it that was just the two of us visiting today. She turned to me and replied, 'No, there was another guy and he looked like you.' It was then that I knew my brother was there with me as I served my mission." Johnny's experience is a reminder that as missionaries God does not leave us alone.

Knowing the pain of loneliness surely strengthens the message of the gospel of Jesus Christ because He has prepared a way for us to always feel loved. Many of the people you teach are alone in so many ways; they have been without hope, without the truth, without the gift of the Holy Ghost, without companionship, and without peace. As you teach and share the message of the gospel of Jesus Christ with the people you teach, I hope you will help them to understand that God is with them. The message you share will illuminate their ability to recognize that God is right there waiting to relieve them of the burden of feeling alone. The gospel of Jesus Christ promises that your friend, the Savior, will be with you always.

Sister Elaine L. Jack told this story in a BYU Women's Conference years ago:

> Our joy and our hope begins and ends in our Savior. A sister expressed to me: "Not long ago I was feeling sorry for myself. I've been struggling to pay bills. Upon retiring to bed one night feeling the worse for the daily battle, I lay in my bed moaning to myself. It was then that I looked up to the picture I have of the Savior on my wall. His eyes seemed to look into my very soul, and at the same time these words came to my mind: 'I am here. I've always been by your side, taking the pain you feel as well. I drank the bitter cup for you and I gladly did so. I love you. I always will and I'll always be here with you every step of the way.'
>
> As tears streamed down my face, I felt like the Savior's arms had circled my body and were hugging me. I felt so secure, so loved and wanted—a feeling I can still feel as I write this on paper. The feeling of loneliness left me immediately."[1]

In the Book of Mormon, Amulek, a recently reactivated member of the Church, shared a powerful insight when he referred to the loving arms of God as "the arms of safety" (Alma 34:16). Alma, who had been retrieved from a dark past by the arms of God in his life, called them "the arms of mercy" (Alma 5:33). When I think of the arms of a loving God, I see arms that elevate, retrieve, carry, protect, strengthen, and support. I am grateful for a loving Father and Savior who will continually extend their "arms of safety" and "arms of mercy" when we feel alone. May you be encircled about in those precious arms as you serve, and may you help others feel the safety of those sacred and loving arms, so that you and those you minister to may never feel alone.

Your friend,
Brother Jeff Erickson

NOTES

1.   Elaine L. Jack, "A Perfect Brightness of Hope," *Ensign*, March 1992.

FILLED

Dear Elders and Sisters,

As a bishop, I remember one Sunday afternoon when I received a knock on my door at home from a member of my ward. A good sister in the ward had just received her patriarchal blessing, and she was filled to overflowing with the Spirit. She wanted to share her amazing experience with her husband, but he was not active, and she knew that he might not understand. She drove around for a while, wondering who she could tell about what had happened to her and what she was feeling. She finally stopped at my house and attempted to explain to me how wonderful her experience receiving a patriarchal blessing was. I spent a few minutes with her, listening to her testimony of what had just occurred. This Spirit-filled experience helped her to move forward in faith and seek to fulfill all those wonderful promises in her blessing.

When most young men and young women leave for a mission, their spiritual tank is probably closer to empty than full. I believe one of the purposes of a full-time mission is for the Lord to fill our tank so full with experiences that those experiences will carry us during the years after we come home. Being spiritually filled seems to help with the transition home and the transition to part-time missionary service. There is nothing better as a missionary than having the Lord fill your cup to overflowing. I would tell you this, when you have finished your mission, make sure you come home with your tank absolutely full. The Lord gives many promises to us about filling us with wonderful spiritual things. I will share a few.

This is one of my favorite promises, and you should share it with all the people you teach: "And it shall come to pass, that whoso repenteth and is baptized in my name shall be filled" (3 Nephi 27:16). The question that should arise is, "Filled with what?" So many wonderful things! The next verses are full of promises that will answer that question:

> "Verily, verily, I say unto you, I will impart unto you of my Spirit, which shall enlighten your mind, which shall fill your soul with joy" (D&C 11:13).

> "And it came to pass that after they had spoken these words the Spirit of the Lord came upon them, and they were filled with joy, having received a remission of their sins, and having peace of conscience, because of the exceeding faith which they had in Jesus Christ who should come" (Mosiah 4:3).

The joy that fills us comes from knowing truth, being forgiven, having light, and understanding the Lord's wonderful and merciful plan.

I remember vividly one of the most sacred days of my life. I got up early and drove to Orem to pick up my fiancée, Christine. We drove north to the Salt Lake Temple. We went inside, and I knew the day would be amazing, but I didn't comprehend how amazing it would be. We got dressed and then went to the sealing room, where many of our friends and family were gathered waiting for us. After some instruction from a wonderful sealer, we knelt at an altar of God to be married and sealed for eternity. When the sealer began the sacred ceremony my heart burst with joy as the Spirit filled my being to overflowing. For the next few minutes, I was completely overcome, and I cried through the ceremony. I was filled with a mixture of gratitude, love, and awe that a loving God would allow me to be sealed to this wonderful woman whom I loved more than life itself. I will never forget how God filled my cup to overflowing on that sacred occasion of my eternal sealing.

Here are more promises about being filled to overflowing:

> "See that ye bridle all your passions, that ye may be filled with love" (Alma 38:12).

> "And also that they might give thanks to the Lord their God . . . who had taught them to keep the commandments of God, that they might rejoice and be filled with love towards God and all men" (Mosiah 2:4).

"The Holy Ghost, which Comforter filleth with hope and perfect love" (Moroni 8:26).

Remember to fill your cup with love because there is no more powerful force in the universe. The attribute of being "filled with love" is the one I think of when I think of Christ.

The Savior said in the Sermon on the Mount, "The light of the body is the eye: if therefore thine eye be single, thy whole body shall be full of light" (Matthew 6:22). Here are some additional promises if our eye is single to the glory of God:

"And if your eye be single to my glory, your whole bodies shall be filled with light, and there shall be no darkness in you; and that body which is filled with light comprehendeth all things" (D&C 88:67).

"All shall be filled with knowledge of the Lord" (D&C 84:98).

"Open your mouths and they shall be filled" (D&C 33:8).

As a missionary, following the example of the sons of Mosiah, "For they were men of a sound understanding and they had searched the scriptures diligently, that they might know the word of God," (Alma 17:2) brings an abundance of light to our life. We know the light will keep the darkness of sin from our lives.

I remember, a few years ago, observing this promised light filling a recent convert in our ward. Brother Martin was the Gospel Doctrine instructor in our ward, and he was a convert of only a few years. He was a joy to observe while he taught because his enthusiasm was infectious. Bob was a brilliant lawyer who loved to study history. On occasion, while he was teaching the Gospel Doctrine class, you could see the pure flow of intelligence and light come over him as he explained a variety of gospel principles. When he would share a newly discovered, profound restored doctrine or principle, his excitement would spill over into his teaching. He would remind those of us who had been members for a long time, how amazing these truths and doctrines were. I can still hear Brother Martin's voice repeating this memorable phrase as he would teach and say, "You people don't know what you have." The gospel filled Brother Martin with light and knowledge.

There has always been a big difference between a returned missionary and one returning filled with the power of God. Here are two phrases that every parent would love to feel and see in their returning son or daughter: "I am filled with the power of God" (1 Nephi 17:48) and "Behold, I am full of the Spirit of God" (1 Nephi 17:47). I don't believe there is a better feeling in the world than being filled with the Spirit. Every significant experience with the Spirit in my life has been memorable.

Years ago, my family was delivering cookies to families during the Christmas season. We sent my young son McKay to one door, and he made the cookie delivery. On his way back to the car, he was running and making big circles with his arms and chanting, "We are spreading joy, we are spreading joy!" I hope you feel what young McKay did, as your message fills both yourself and the people you teach. I hope when you reflect upon your missionary service that you feel as the Psalmist did: "Thou preparest a table before me in the presence of mine enemies: thou anointest my head with oil; my cup runneth over" (Psalm 23:5). Finally, as you depart each area after a transfer, may your "cup runneth over" as you think of the people you taught, the less-actives you inspired, and the treasured experiences you have had with your companions and in your sector. May you feel as Ammon did when he saw his friends and fellow missionaries who also had been serving the Lord: "Now the joy of Ammon was so great even that he was full; yea, he was swallowed up in the joy of his God, even to the exhausting of his strength; and he fell again to the earth. Now was not this exceeding joy? Behold, this is joy which none receiveth save it be the truly penitent and humble seeker of happiness." (Alma 27:17–18)

May you, as a humble servant and a humble seeker of happiness, be filled.

Your friend,
Brother Jeff Erickson

THE SPIRIT WILL NOT FAIL US

Dear Elders and Sisters,

Elder Franklin D. Richards shared this story about a young cadet:

I recall a testimony given by a young cadet attending the United States Air Force Academy.

He was experiencing great difficulty in passing his courses and was very discouraged. At this point, he met a Mormon cadet, and from him he learned that there were a number of Mormon boys attending the academy and that they met together at five o'clock each weekday morning in a religious study class. The cadet was invited to attend one of these classes.

He did so and was deeply impressed by the wonderful spirit. He continued attending, met the missionaries, was given the missionary lessons, and, through study, prayer, and attending church, received a testimony and was baptized.

He bore witness that upon receiving the Holy Ghost he felt its influence quicken his mind and understanding and refresh his memory, and that thereafter he had no trouble in getting satisfactory grades. His feelings of discouragement left him, and a spirit of peace and comfort came over him. This was a most inspiring and impressive testimony of the great value of the Holy Ghost."[1]

This young man's experience is a powerful reminder that the Holy Ghost will never fail us in our righteous efforts. Today, I have a wonderful principle to share with you. It is taught in the fourth chapter of Alma, and may you always remember it as a missionary. This was a trying time for Alma. A huge and exhausting war had just ended. He came home and had some wonderful missionary success, but it seemed to be thwarted by so much iniquity. Alma retired from his role as high priest and became a full-time minister. He then went on a mission to

THE SPIRIT WILL NOT FAIL US

all the cities in the Church. I can feel the weight of Alma's burdens as I read this verse: "And now it came to pass that Alma, having seen the afflictions of the humble followers of God, and the persecutions which were heaped upon them by the remainder of his people, and seeing all their inequality, began to be very sorrowful; nevertheless the Spirit of the Lord did not fail him" (Alma 4:15). This verse becomes a powerful testimony that the Spirit of God will never fail us if we do our part.

I am certain that Alma was weighed down and discouraged, but it was the Spirit of the Lord that carried him. He went from city to city and had remarkable experiences as the Spirit of the Lord guided and directed him as to what he should teach. Alma experienced what Nephi taught, "Do ye not remember that I said unto you that after ye had received the Holy Ghost ye could speak with the tongue of angels? And now, how could ye speak with the tongue of angels save it were by the Holy Ghost?" (2 Nephi 32:2). The Spirit of the Lord will not fail missionaries, and it will allow them to testify with the tongue of angels.

There are times in our missions when we will be discouraged and frustrated and lose some hope, but remember that the Spirit of the Lord will not fail us. "When our time is spent in the accumulation of experiences that nourish the Spirit, we see with different glasses things that others do not see and cannot understand."[2]

A year ago, I was sitting in deacons quorum for what I thought was going to be a rather typical class. I was teaching the lesson on the Restoration of the gospel. We were reading verses seven through twenty in Joseph Smith—History as a group. We stopped to discuss verses as needed. We had been going around the room in a circle taking turns reading. We had just finished verse seventeen, and there was a wonderful spirit in the room. It was now Brother Rogers's, one of our Scoutmasters, turn to read. He had been paying close attention, and the Spirit settled upon him in a marvelous way as he heard the precious words from verse seventeen: "When the light rested upon me I saw two Personages, whose brightness and glory defy all description, standing above me in the air. One of them spake unto me, calling me by name and said, pointing to the other—This is My Beloved Son. Hear Him!" (Joseph Smith—History 1:17).

Brother Rogers attempted to begin verse eighteen, but couldn't even get started because the Spirit overwhelmed him. After a very spiritual and intense few moments, he let the Spirit settle in him and, through his tears, slowly finished the verse. I knew that he knew that what Joseph saw and experienced was real. Brother Rogers already knew that Joseph Smith was a prophet, but that day the Spirit reaffirmed it to him. A group of young deacons felt the intense spirit of the message of Joseph Smith that day, maybe for the first time. The Spirit testified to them of the divine calling of the prophet Joseph Smith. As we all walked out of our deacons quorum class, the Spirit had not failed us, but had strengthened our testimony of the prophet Joseph Smith and enlightened our minds. With enlightened minds and hearts, we could all say, "Joseph Smith is a prophet of God because the Spirit of God told us so."

God said, "Pray always, and I will pour out my Spirit upon you, and great shall be your blessing" (D&C 19:38). Your blessings will be great as you rely on and depend upon the Spirit of God. Remember, Nephi taught this critical principle early in the Book of Mormon: "And I was led by the Spirit, not knowing beforehand the things which I should do" (1 Nephi 4:6). We don't always know why investigators don't progress or why people don't listen or why people continue in their evil ways, but when the Spirit leads us, the Lord will guide our words and actions.

Depend on the Spirit. Pray for Him, plead for Him, and let Him guide your actions, words, decisions, and directions. Elder Bruce R. McConkie taught, "There is *no limit* to the revelations [we] may receive"[3] Remember the sons of Mosiah:

And they went forth whithersoever they were led by the Spirit of the Lord, preaching the word of God in every synagogue of the Amalekites, or in every assembly of the Lamanites where they could be admitted.

And it came to pass that the Lord began to bless them, insomuch that they brought many to the knowledge of the truth; yea, they did convince many of their sins, and of the traditions of their fathers, which were not correct. (Alma 21:16–17)

Those are the same promises we have when the Spirit leads us today. The Spirit will not fail us if we do our part. Alma taught us that everyone has the same opportunity, no matter their mission or area, and it really comes down to receptiveness to the Spirit.

"And thus they have been called to this holy calling on account of their faith, while others would reject the Spirit of God on account of the hardness of their hearts and blindness of their minds, while, if it had not been for this they might have had as great privilege as their brethren" (Alma 13:4). Privilege comes by righteousness, and the Spirit leads us as we pray always and are faithful. No matter the companion, area, or mission, the Lord promises: "And whoso receiveth you, there I will be also, for I will go before your face. I will be on your right hand and on your left, and my Spirit shall be in your hearts, and mine angels round about you, to bear you up" (D&C 84:88).

I remember as a full-time missionary teaching a young man named Ernie. He had not been very interested in our message, but had committed to listening to the lessons. He endured the first lesson, but something happened during the second lesson that was completely foreign to Ernie. We were teaching the plan of salvation when the presence of the Spirit blanketed this young man and my companion and I watched his countenance change. I stopped the lesson to help Ernie identify what he was feeling. I said, "Ernie, do you feel that?" Almost shouting, he said, "Yeah, what is that?" I explained that it was the Holy Ghost testifying to him that the message was true. He said, "I have never felt that before." The Spirit did not fail us that day.

The Spirit will lift you from despair. He will strengthen you during trials, fill your heart with courage and power, and carry you through the darkest of times. I promise you that as hope wavers, as investigators break commitments, and as despair comes, that the light and power of the Holy Ghost will never fail you as you faithfully serve the Lord. "And it came to pass that the Lord did visit them with his Spirit, and said unto them: Be comforted. And they were comforted" (Alma 17:10). May the Spirit comfort you when you need His sacred influence.

Your friend,
Brother Jeff Erickson

Remember, You Are Not Alone

NOTES

1.   Franklin D. Richards, "The Continuing Power of the Holy Ghost," *Ensign*, July 1973.

2.   Ardeth G. Kapp, "What Will You Make Room for in Your Wagon," *BYU Speeches*, November 13, 1990.

3.   Bruce R. McConkie *A New Witness for the Articles of Faith* (Salt Lake City: Deseret Book, 1985), 490, quoted in Sheri L. Dew, "You Were Born to Lead, You Were Born for Glory," *BYU Speeches*, December 9, 2003; emphasis in original.

LOVE THE PEOPLE

Dear Elders and Sisters,

I wanted to write today about the power of loving the people you serve. We learn from Mormon that "charity never faileth" (Moroni 7:46). I have often wondered what Mormon means when he says "never." There is an amazing power and promise in that doctrine of charity. Love is the basis of the gospel of Jesus Christ. Love is what motivated the plan and the Atonement. Love is what changes hearts and inspires and motivates people to change. Here are a few stories about the power of Christlike love.

Barbara B. Smith, a former General President of the Relief Society, told this story many years ago:

> One evening as I conversed with President Harold B Lee, I said to him, "President Lee, you seem different some way. He smiled and said, "You know what it is, don't you?" I shook my head and said that I really didn't know. Then he shared with me this remarkable experience. "After I became the President of the Church . . . one night when I was sleeping, President David O. McKay came to me in a dream. He pointed his finger and looked at me with those piercing eyes of his as only President McKay could do, and he said, 'If you want to love God, you have to learn to love and serve the people. That is the way you show your love for God' . . . That's what you can feel, it is my newfound ability to truly love and serve his children."[1]

There is a story of a man who took great pride in his lawn and was upset when he found himself with a large crop of dandelions. He tried every method he knew of to get rid of them. Still they plagued him. Finally, he wrote the Department of Agriculture. He enumerated all the things he had tried and asked what else he could do. In due course, the reply came: "We suggest that you learn to love your dandelions."[2] There is great power in loving things or people who are different. When we see beyond our limits, we really see. When we love others, we truly begin to see as God sees.

A few months ago, my son Taft was going next door to borrow some ingredients to make some cookies on a Sunday. He received the ingredients from our neighbor Steve and then, out of habit, said, "Thanks, I love you." He came home giggling at what he had done. A few minutes later, I received a text from Steve that said, "Tell Taft I love him too." If we are going to error in life, or as missionaries, may it be in love and kindness rather than dissension, anger, or apathy.

Here is a simple daily event shared by H. Burke Peterson, a former general authority.

> Two weeks ago President Kimball passed me as we were rushing to a meeting. He stopped, took my hand, looked me in the eye, put away all of his other cares, and said simply, "I'm sorry we're sometimes so busy. I guess I haven't told you lately how much I love you and appreciate you."
>
> I felt his spirit; I believed him; my spirit soared to a new height.[3]

Elder Boyd K. Packer shared the following experience:

> I recall on one occasion, when I was returning from seminary to my home for lunch, that as I drove in, my wife met me in the driveway. I could tell by the expression on her face that something was wrong. "Cliff has been killed," she said. "They want you to come over." As I hastened around the corner to where Cliff lived with his wife and four sons and his little daughter, I saw Cliff lying in the middle of the highway with a blanket over him. The ambulance was just pulling away with little Colleen. Cliff had been on his way out to the farm and had stopped to cross the street to take little Colleen to her mother, who waited on the opposite curb. But the child, as children will, broke from her father's hand and slipped into the street. A large truck was coming. Cliff jumped from the curb and pushed his little daughter from the path of the truck—but he wasn't soon enough.
>
> A few days later I had the responsibility of talking at the funeral of Cliff and little Colleen. Someone said, "What a terrible waste. Certainly he ought to have stayed on the curb. He knew the child might have died. But he had four sons and a wife to provide for. What a pathetic waste!" And I estimated that that individual never had had the experience of loving someone more than he loved himself.[4]

As you serve the people of your mission, I pray that you will learn to love those people more than you love yourself. As you do, your entire life will be changed. You will learn as the Savior said, "Greater love hath no man than this, that a man lay down his life for a friend" (John 15:13). For eighteen months or two years, you are setting aside, or laying down your life, for your friends, your loved ones, and your God. May you find joy and happiness and love in doing so.

Your friend,
Brother Jeff Erickson

It's All about Love

NOTES

1.   B. Kelly, *Harold B. Lee: A Dramatized History* (Covenant Communications, 2001), audio CD.
2.   Marc Foley, *Story of a Soul: The Autobiography of St. Thérèse of Lisieux,* trans. John Clarke, 3rd ed. (Washington, D.C.: ICS Publications, 2005), 41.
3.   H. Burke Peterson, "The Daily Portion of Love," *Ensign*, May 1977.
4.   Ted L. Gibbons, *Be Not Afraid: Turning to Christ in Times of Crisis* (Springville, Utah: Cedar Fort, 2009), 19–20.

WORTH OF A SOUL

Dear Elders and Sisters,

Over a year ago, a family in our ward introduced a man named Rene to the gospel of Jesus Christ. Rene had been very active in his church for many years, and he was very content with his religion. His first exposure to the Church was the First Presidency Christmas broadcast where he heard President Thomas S. Monson speak. Rene said when he heard President Monson speak, he felt something. The missionaries began to teach Rene, and his experience and personal change was remarkable and wonderful. Rene heard the plan of salvation and couldn't believe how wonderful it was. He embraced all the truths of the gospel as they were taught to him. The missionaries built on the wonderful religious foundation that he already had. A few weeks later, Rene was baptized.

Rene is in his fifties, but he has the enthusiasm and excitement of a twenty-year-old when it comes to the gospel of Jesus Christ. A few days ago, I received a phone call from Rene. He said, "I love this Church and being a part of it, it means the world to me, and I am going to tell everyone that I love it. I am speaking in stake conference, and I am going to tell everyone what a blessing the gospel is, and I just want to thank you for your role in my life." I really did not do much, but I did help a tiny bit in this good brother's search for truth. This much I know, when I got off the phone, I rejoiced in this his happiness, blessings, and wonderful testimony. I rejoiced that he had been found.

My message today is a reminder of the tremendous value of the one soul that you may be teaching, mentoring, or reactivating. I don't know if there is a better parable in all of scripture than the parable of the lost sheep. In Luke 15, the Savior teaches us so many powerful lessons with one wonderful metaphor for the value of every soul. He asked, "What man of you, having an hundred sheep, if he lose one of them, doth not leave the ninety and nine in the wilderness, and go after that which is lost, until he find it?" (Luke 15:4). There are a few powerful words and phrases in that verse. I will focus on two words and one phrase. The phrase is "go after," which to me implies a sense of boldness—not waiting, not just sowing, not being complacent, but acting deliberately. "Go after" means to testify, invite, and earnestly seek and find instead of sitting in an apartment waiting for a phone call. The gospel is about searching for the elect. It's about opening our mouths and "[sparing] not" (D&C 33:9). Sharing the gospel is not for the passive or the faint of heart; it is for those who truly want to rescue the Lord's sheep.

The first word I want to discuss in Luke 15:4, is "one." Our Heavenly Father and our Savior have always emphasized the worth of every individual soul. They have never been about numbers, but about individuals. For example, "And if it so be that you should labor all your days in crying repentance unto this people, and bring, save it be one soul unto me, how great shall be your joy with him in the kingdom of my Father!" (D&C 18:15). Years ago, Elder Marvin J. Ashton said, "In God's eyes, nobody is a nobody."[1] Remember, if you help to save just one, you have been a savior to that one. God loves all of His children.

One of the saddest interviews of my life changed my course forever. I was meeting with a wonderful lady who was struggling with her self-worth. We talked of many concerns and struggles. At one point, she said very honestly, "There isn't a single person that cares about me." When I heard her words, I felt that she really believed what she was saying. Hearing those personal thoughts, through her tears, haunted me and still haunts me to this day. Her comments made me want to be someone who finds and ministers to the one. I wanted her to know so desperately that God loves her more than she could ever imagine. Her words reminded me of how important the work you do as a full-time missionary is. You must find those who need and yearn to feel the love of our Heavenly Father.

I have always loved this story about the importance of each of us: "Sir Michael Costa, a famous conductor, was rehearsing with a vast array of performers and hundreds of voices, the piccolo player far up in

It's All about Love

the corner ceased to play, thinking within all the chorus and orchestra his instrument would not be missed. Suddenly the great conductor stopped and threw up his hands and all was silent. Then he cried out, 'where is the piccolo?'"[2] Every one of Heavenly Father's children needs to feel His presence and partake of His love.

The second word in Luke 15:4 that I find hope in is the preposition "until." The role of a preposition is to link things together. The word "until" signifies that we are linked to the Savior, no matter how far away or how lost we are. The word "until" reminds me that the Savior would search for me without ever giving up. If I am elect and prepared, and I want to follow the Good Shepherd, He will find me or send one of His emissaries to find me. I know He would have us emulate Him by searching for the lost sheep until we find them. There is great satisfaction in knowing that everyone that should be found will be found if we continue in the search.

The next few verses are full of great foresight because they denote success and the joy that comes when you find and assist the one:

> And when he hath found it, he layeth it on his shoulders, rejoicing.
>
> And when he cometh home, he calleth together his friends and neighbours, saying unto them, Rejoice with me; for I have found my sheep which was lost.
>
> I say unto you, that likewise joy shall be in heaven over one sinner that repenteth. (Luke 15:5–7)

I look back at missionary successes in finding souls, and in every case, there has been rejoicing. This doesn't mean that the effort was always complete or lasting, but for those who repented, the joy was immense and heartfelt. I testify I have felt what this parable teaches. I am grateful for the Rene's of the world who remind me of the joy of searching until we find those precious souls.

In 1888, a Dutch artist painted a landscape painting called "Sunset At Montmajour." He was not very happy with his efforts and never signed the painting. Eventually, the painting was sold to Christian Nicolai Mustad, who showed it in his home. He thought it might be an authentic painting of the famed Vincent van Gogh. He was told by a guest that it was not authentic. Mustad took down the painting and put it in his attic. He eventually died, and years later, the new owners

WORTH OF A SOUL

of the painting took it to the Van Gogh Museum in 1991, and it was evaluated as not an authentic Van Gogh.

In 2013, these same persistent owners took the painting back to the Van Gogh Museum. Over the last twenty years, there have been new techniques and processes discovered that are available to help evaluate authenticity, and these new techniques were used. This time, with new technology and a critical letter from Vincent van Gogh to his brother, the painting was authenticated. The painting's value is now estimated in the fifty million dollar range.[3]

The people you are teaching are similar to this precious painting. They are of infinite worth, but they need to discover their worth and their value. Your role as a representative of Christ is to help them discover how authentic they are. You are to help them understand how real the plan is and how these values and standards will change their life. Many precious souls are figuratively "left in the attic" of not knowing, but are waiting to be found. Missionaries need to find them and help them discover their tremendous value.

As you search for lost sheep, remember Alma's words to Corianton, "Behold, I say unto you, is not a soul at this time as precious unto God as a soul will be at the time of his coming" (Alma 39:17). May you continue to search and rejoice as you find those precious sheep.

Your friend,
Brother Jeff Erickson

NOTES

1. Marvin J. Ashton, "While They Are Waiting," *Ensign*, May 1988.
2. J. Randolph Ayre, *Illustrations to Inspire* (Bookcraft, 1968), 8.
3. Nina Siegal, "A van Gogh's Trip From the Attic to the Museum," *The New York Times*, September 9, 2013.

167

CHARITY NEVER FAILS

Dear Elders and Sisters,

Elder Marvin J. Ashton shared this experience: "A friend of mine recently shared what he considered to be a choice learning experience. It was provided by his young son. Upon returning home from his day's work, this father greeted his boy with a pat on the head and said, 'Son, I want you to know I love you.' The son responded with, 'Oh Dad, I don't want you to love me, I want you to play football with me.' Here was a boy conveying a much-needed message."[1] Every missionary needs to know that there is power in words, but that there is much greater power in Christlike love.

There is one principle that will help a young man or young woman to never fail as a missionary. No matter where a missionary serves or how hard the area or mission, if they follow this critical piece of advice from Mormon, they will always succeed. Mormon said, "Wherefore, my beloved brethren, if ye have not charity, ye are nothing, *for charity never faileth*. Wherefore, cleave unto charity, which is the greatest of all, for all things must fail" (Moroni 7:46; emphasis added).

I believe the principle that charity never fails is true. The pure love of Christ motivates, inspires, and changes hearts. Missionaries who truly feel the pure love of Christ for the people of their mission are always successful. They always leave an impression on the people around them, whether they convert them or not.

How do you obtain charity? It really is by how you act and how well you submit to Heavenly Father. Some people lack the attributes of charity and wonder why people don't believe their message. To that I say, you can't teach what you don't live. The gospel is a message of absolute charity from the master of charity, Jesus Christ.

One of the great demonstrations of charity is found in the life of Ammon, as he faithfully served King Lamoni in the Book of Mormon. The servants of the king return from the waters of Sebus and tell the king of Ammon's faithfulness and great power in defending the king's flocks. The scriptures tell us the king was "astonished" (Alma 18:2). The king asks, "Where is this man that has such great power?" (Alma 18:8). Where is he? He is out fulfilling his duty to the king. The king calls Ammon to come unto him. Then Ammon stands before him for an hour, and the king just looks at him and marvels. There are so many things he could have been thinking, but something had stirred in his soul. He was so impressed with Ammon's qualities, faithfulness, exactness, courage, discernment, and Christlike power. He even thought that Ammon might be the Great Spirit—what a compliment to Ammon's Christlike qualities!

Finally, Ammon asks, "Wilt thou hearken unto my words, if I tell thee by what power I do these things?" (Alma 18:22). The lesson is in the next verse when Lamoni says, "Yea, I will believe all thy words" (Alma 18:23). Wow! What does that mean? He knew that Ammon would speak the truth. With Lamoni's experience, charity never failed. Charity conquered every barrier. The king was a bad man, but every ounce of evil was removed from him through Ammon's charity. I pray that you will have experiences, like Ammon's, where people say, "The way you live is true, it is inspiring, and I want to know for myself what you know for yourself."

What is charity to a missionary? "And charity suffereth long, and is kind, and envieth not, and is not puffed up, seeketh not her own, is not easily provoked, thinketh no evil, and rejoiceth not in iniquity but rejoiceth in the truth, beareth all things, believeth all things, hopeth all things, endureth all things" (Moroni 7:45). As a missionary, are you suffering with people? Are you patient with your companion, people that don't agree with you, or investigators who don't progress fast enough? Do you understand that the Lord will provide in His appointed time? Are you kind? Do you genuinely care about the people you minister to and serve? Do you envy the skills of your companion? Do you long to be in an area where other missionaries are having so much success? Do you feel like the Lord shortchanged you on talents and gifts? Are you proud? That is a broad word, as pride can be manifested in so many different ways. Pride really is the stumbling block for missionaries as it causes them to lose charity, to make fun or light of others, to judge others unrighteously, or to lift themselves above others.

Do you seek your own? Are you worried about how you look to other missionaries? Are you worrying about leadership and making sure people know how great you are, or are you just worried about the message and proclaiming it? Are you easily provoked? Do you get upset when you are rejected? Are you short tempered with your companion or disinterested people? Do those who reject your message easily offend you? Are you quick to think bad thoughts about someone who turns you away? Are you quietly and patiently waiting upon the Lord and His goodness?

What do you think about? Do you have bad or unclean thoughts? Do you dwell mentally on things that are not appropriate? Do you focus on Christ and the plan? There is something wonderful about clearing your mind and having thoughts that are filled with charity, faith, and hope. Do you stay away from rejoicing in past iniquities? Do you share past sins with companions? Do you listen excitedly to their sins, or have you put your hand to the plow and not looked back? (See Luke 9:62.) Don't dwell in Babylon—you have already left there. Put off the natural man and become a saint.

Do you rejoice in the truth? Do you love your message? Do you want to proclaim it from the rooftops? Are you like Alma and wish you were an angel whose voice could be like a trump? Do you personally love living the gospel because of the peace and happiness it brings?

The aspect of charity "that beareth all things, believeth all things, hopeth all things, and endureth all things" is living the gospel at all costs. It is knowing the path but understanding that it is an arduous road. It is knowing that the devil's mighty winds will beat against you, but if you continue to walk the strait and narrow you will reach the destination. It is knowing the path is perfect, but that the journey will be filled with difficulty. It is saying "thy will be done" (Matthew 26:42), whatever His will is. Charity will never fail because God said so. It is the one divine attribute we must have to inherit celestial glory. Charity is the attribute that will make all the difference as you teach, testify, and proclaim the gospel of Jesus Christ. Charity is what made it possible for our Savior to do the things he accomplished. Charity is truly what brought about the Atonement of Jesus Christ. May you never fail as you faithfully serve Heavenly Father.

As a bishop, I had the privilege of interviewing every seven-year-old just before they turned eight. This interview was a baptismal interview where I would ask a lot of questions and attempt to teach them about the blessings of baptism and the importance of the proper priesthood administering the ordinance. Little Abbie was in one of these interviews when I asked her why she wanted to be baptized. She shared some good reasons. I then asked her, "Who do you want to baptize you?" She replied, "My dad." I said that would be wonderful—he would like that. I was now going to teach young Abbie about the priesthood, so I asked another follow-up question: "Abbie, why do you want your dad to baptize you?" I was hoping she would say, "Because he has the priesthood." Instead, she powerfully taught me an important lesson as she thoughtfully said, "Because I love him." Abbie reminded me, out of the mouth of a babe, that the most powerful influence in the world will always be the pure love of Christ.

Your friend,
Brother Jeff Erickson

It's All about Love

NOTES

1. Marvin J. Ashton, "Love Takes Time," *Ensign*, November 1975.

COMPANIONSHIPS

Dear Elders and Sisters,

I wanted to speak of companion relationships. A few years ago, my wife and I taught a marriage class in our ward. We hoped the class would bless many with a desire to strengthen their marriages. The companionship of marriage is obviously different than missionary companionships, but in many ways, it is similar to having a companion in the mission field. In reality, there is probably no better preparation for marriage than having fifteen different companions from different walks of life, cultures, and social climates.

I believe it is easy to be selfish and not care about your companion. It is often difficult to put someone else first. A mission teaches you how to do that. This type of selflessness is only accomplished through much effort and sacrifice. If you can be a selfless companion, even with the tough elders or sisters, you will be a great husband or wife. If you never learn to do the little things for your companions, you will never do them for your future spouse. If you compete with your companion, you will compete with your spouse. You can't be a selfish companion for eighteen months or two years and come home and be an unselfish husband or wife.

I remember one compelling experience I had late in my mission with a new companion. I was assigned on a transfer to serve with a companion that I was not excited about. I knew I needed to repent and change my attitude and approach. I made a commitment that I would pray daily to have love for him, and then I would make a concentrated effort to love him. The plan actually surprised me as it worked wonderfully. It was one of the best months of my mission. When I was transferred, I was disappointed because he had become a true friend and a

On the left margin: It's All about Love

great companion. Our differences had complemented one another, and the Lord had blessed us with many memorable experiences. For me, it was a great lesson in learning how to be a good companion and a true friend.

There is tremendous power in a companionship working and serving the Lord together as one. President Boyd K. Packer, former President of the Quorum of the Twelve Apostles, once attended an ox-pulling contest at a country fair in New Hampshire, where he drew out an analogy. He said of the experience:

> The center of attraction was the oxen-pulling contest. Several teams of oxen with heavy wooden yokes were lined up to compete. A wooden sledge was weighted with cement blocks: ten thousand pounds—five tons—to begin with. The object was for the oxen to move the sledge three feet.
>
> I noticed a well-matched pair of very large, brindled, blue-gray animals. They were the big-boned, Holstein, Durham-cross, familiar big blue oxen of seasons past. Because of their size, of course they were the favorites.
>
> Each team was given three attempts to move the sledge. If they were able to do so easily, more weight was added until the teams were eliminated one by one. In turn, each team was hitched to the sledge. The teamster would position his animals carefully, pat them, chortle to them, whisper to them, and then at a goad and a loud command they would slam forward against the yoke. Either the weight would move or the oxen were jerked to a halt.
>
> The big blue oxen didn't even place! A small, nondescript pair of animals, not very well matched for size, moved the sledge all three times.
>
> I was amazed and fascinated and turned to an old New Englander in the crowd and asked if he could explain how that could happen. He said, "E-yeh." (That means yes in New England.) And then he explained. The big blues were larger and stronger and better matched for size than the other team. But the little oxen had better teamwork and coordination. They hit the yoke together. Both animals jerked forward at exactly the same time and the force moved the load.[1]

May you and your companions be yoked together in moving forward the work of God with a oneness of heart, mind, and strength. Love is life's greatest motivator. How does Christ motivate us to serve and sacrifice? Through the love He shows and shares with us. Why are

It's All about Love

His words and impressions so powerful? They are all an act of love for us. When we feel the Spirit, that is a wonderful act of love to remind us that as we teach we know that He loves the people we teach. Love is really what the gospel of Jesus Christ is all about. Mormon says it wonderfully in Moroni 7:46—"charity never faileth."

Here are a few of the principles my wife and I taught in the last lesson for our ward marriage class that will hopefully be a blessing to you in your companionships. I hope you will be able to see the parallel in these marital principles.

1. Selfishness is the number one cause of divorce; thus, it must be the number one cause of poor companionships.
2. Love the one you're with. You have your mission companion for a set time; don't wish away the weeks. Make the most of the short time you have together.
3. Find out what is important to them and take an interest in that.

Remember, as Mormon said, true love will not fail you. May you heed Pahoran's advice when he said to Moroni, "See that ye strengthen Lehi and Teancum in the Lord" (Alma 61:21). I know there can be some impossible companions, but love will always make things better. I know that many of your companions would never be your friends at home, but it is far greater to make friends than enemies. Your life will be blessed with fond memories of your companions that you can reflect on for years. Don't fill those memories with could have's and should have's.

As you approach your companionships during your mission, may I suggest the approach of Lenny Skutnik. Lenny was a bystander when Air Florida flight 90 left the Washington National Airport on January 13, 1982. The plane struggled on take-off and hit the 14th Street Bridge before plunging into the icy Potomac River. The plane sank quickly as debris spilled across the water. There were a few survivors floating in the icy water where the tail of the plane had broken off. Time was short for any rescue attempt as the temperature of the water only left minutes for survival. A local park police helicopter was attempting to carry survivors from the plane's tail to the shoreline with a simple rope. One survivor, Priscilla Tirado, had been carried thirty feet from shore when she no longer had the strength to hang on to the rope. Lenny Skutnik and hundreds of others, even rescue workers, watched, almost paralyzed, from the bridge and from the shoreline. Priscilla struggled in the frigid waters and called out for help. That's when Lenny finally took action. He took off his coat and boots, jumped into the river, and swam to her aid in the bone-chilling waters. He finally reached her, and dragged her back to the safety of the shoreline.[2]

Lenny was hailed as a hero for his courageous actions. May you go and do likewise. Don't just watch a struggling companion; rather, jump in and immerse yourself in helping through service, teaching, training, inspiring, and enriching your companionship. Do all you can to help them, aid them, and rescue them as needed. Your courage, involvement, interest, and efforts will forever be appreciated by those companions who knew you loved them and knew you would sacrifice anything for them.

When I read Helaman's letter to Captain Moroni, I am reminded of the power of a true friendship or companionship: "And these are the words which he wrote, saying: My dearly beloved brother, Moroni, as well in the Lord as in the tribulations of our warfare; behold, my beloved brother, I have somewhat to tell you concerning our warfare in this part of the land" (Alma 56:2). What a blessing if we can all sincerely address all our companions as our "dearly beloved brother [or sister]."

Your friend,
Brother Jeff Erickson

NOTES

1.   Boyd K. Packer, "Equally Yoked Together," address delivered at regional representatives' seminar, April 3, 1975, in *Teaching Seminary: Preservice Readings* (Salt Lake City: The Church of Jesus Christ of Latter-day Saints, 2004), 30.
2.   Sue Anne Pressley Montes, "In a Moment of Horror, Rousing Acts of Courage," *The Washington Post*, January 13, 2007.

WALLS OF STONE

Dear Elders and Sisters,

The *Iliad,* written by Homer, tells the powerful story of the Trojan War. The Greeks sailed one thousand ships across the Aegean Sea with thousands of men to lay siege to Troy. Troy was a well-fortified city. The Trojans were noted for their industry and ability as warriors. For ten years, the amazing warriors of Troy resisted the overwhelming Greek force. The walled city appeared to be unconquerable, and the Greeks were discouraged and ready to return home. However, there was one certainty; Troy was safe as long as they kept the Greeks outside their walls.

The Greeks placed their final hopes on the Trojan Horse. They felt the horse was the one way to get inside the walled city. The Trojan's were told that the horse outside of their walls would bring continual misfortune, but if they brought it in, it would lose its power to harm them. The horse was too big to fit through the gates, so the Trojans took down a section of their wall to bring the horse inside the city. Once inside the walls, the Greeks hidden in the horse, came out and overpowered the guards. They opened the city gates, and the Greek soldiers, now inside the city walls, slew the Trojans and burned the city to the ground. The Trojans had only taken down a small section of their wall, but the wall had been their protection.

I hope that as missionaries with your many assignments, commitments, and workloads, that you are still taking time to fortify yourself. No matter who we are, we must continue to protect ourselves from the adversary. Captain Moroni teaches us tremendous lessons in fortifying ourselves against the ever-present adversary. We read in Alma, "And now it came to pass that Moroni did not stop making preparations for war, or to defend his people against the Lamanites" (Alma 50:1). Moroni was wise beyond his years. Even in times of peace, he did not stop preparing to fight his adversary (the Lamanites). Many missionaries feel they are protected simply because they are missionaries. Remember, your protection will always come because of personal preparation. I love that Moroni "did not stop" making preparations. In regards to reading our scriptures daily, we should not stop. We should not stop our fervent prayers; we should not stop our diligent study or faithful obedience, even when things are going great. The adversary will come again and we must be prepared.

When the Lamanites came again against Captain Moroni and his armies, the enemy was "astonished exceedingly" at the level of fortification (Alma 49:5). They could not believe how prepared the Nephites were "in preparing their places of security" (Alma 49:5). As missionaries, what are our places of security? They are our rooms where we kneel and read every day and our apartments where we write in our personal and scripture journals. They are the homes we teach in, the sofas we teach from, and the carpets we kneel on after we teach. They are the places we tract, the places we testify, the meetinghouses where we bring less-actives and investigators, the baptismal fonts, and any place where sacred and faith-promoting experiences are had. These are "places of security" for the testifying missionary. These places are made strong by the spirituality and preparation of the missionary and the companionship. Truly it is "wisdom" to maintain and preserve these places of security (Alma 49:5).

I believe Alma 48 teaches us Moroni's philosophy in battling the adversary. We are battling against sin and evil, and Moroni was "preparing to support their liberty" in every area or sector he went (Alma 48:10). We preserve liberty and freedom by overcoming the adversary as well as sin. Here is what Moroni did in every city to preserve peace and liberty: "Yea, he had been strengthening the armies of the Nephites, and erecting small forts, or places of resort; throwing up banks of earth round about to enclose his armies, and also building walls of stone to encircle them about, round about their cities and the borders of their lands; yea, all round about the land" (Alma 48:8). This is one of the best verses about fortification in all of scripture. As a missionary, how can you continue to succeed, work hard, and be obedient?

Finding Strength beyond Your Own

This can be accomplished by erecting "places of resort" and "building walls of stone."

How do we build walls of stone to encircle us and protect us? They must be strong and high, so the darts of the adversary can never penetrate them. I have witnessed that when those walls are weak and shallow, they are very permeable. Missionaries and members who do not labor in strengthening those walls are easily wounded and harmed by the constant onslaught of those damaging darts. Building stone walls high and strong is done through consistency and steadiness. (See Alma 39:1.) I believe walls of stone are built of the materials of daily fervent prayer, meaningful daily scripture study, faithful service, exact obedience, and personal faithfulness. Regular temple attendance also strengthens those walls, but that is usually not possible during full-time missionary service. As a missionary, make sure you are reading daily—at least the mission minimum. Make sure you are prayerful and sincere in your prayers. Make sure you serve at least the minimum hours of teaching and finding. Make sure you "perform every word of command" of the mission president "with exactness" (Alma 57:21). As I say these things, I know there are no missionaries who are perfect, but please be guilty of being overzealous, rather than under-zealous. You will be protected by a loving Heavenly Father as you fortify yourself by building stone walls, and having your places of resort and places of security. Alma said to "watch and pray continually, that ye may not be tempted above that which ye can bear" (Alma 13:28).

May you feel and witness the blessings of this wonderful promise from Jacob as you build your walls: "Wherefore, the people of Nephi did fortify against them with their arms, and with all their might, trusting in the God and rock of their salvation; wherefore, they became as yet, conquerors of their enemies" (Jacob 7:25).

Your friend
Brother Jeff Erickson

Finding Strength
beyond Your Own

"BUT THERE WAS ONE"

Dear Elders and Sisters,

There is a powerful painting done by Carl Bloch of Peter just after his denial of the Savior before His Crucifixion. In the foreground of the painting, Peter is standing in front of the high priest's house. There is also a maid in the foreground, pointing accusingly at Peter denoting that he had been with Christ. Peter's image is unforgettable as his head hangs down, and he looks away. In the background, is the Savior surrounded by soldiers and others being marched away to trial.[1]

When I recently viewed the painting, it was not with an attitude of condemning Peter, but the work inspired me to be more courageous. Looking at the scene, I felt a call to stand firm in behalf of Christ and His principles. This inspiring work of art was a reminder to me that courage is one of the most powerful and necessary Christlike attributes for us to obtain.

A few years ago, my wife and I were sitting in the home of our stake patriarch for one of our son's patriarchal blessings. When the patriarch laid his hands on my son's head and pronounced a blessing, the Spirit filled the room. During the blessing, he bestowed upon my son the gift of courage. When I heard this promise, my heart was immediately filled with joy. In many respects, I was content to feel no other blessings needed to be stated, for if my son had the gift of courage he could do anything. I am deeply grateful that the Lord has bestowed such a powerful gift upon my boy for it will be needed in his life and during these last days.

Today, I write to you about one of my favorite verses in the scriptures. There are so many lessons about courage in this one verse. If there was a verse I would love to be written about me, this is certainly

Finding Strength beyond Your Own

one I would choose. If there is a gift I have prayed for most it would probably be the gift of courage, coming in tied with charity. Courage is earned more than it is given. I think this verse shows the powerful courage of one man.

To understand the verse, you must know what happened before. Abinadi had been testifying to the priests of King Noah. He had been filled with the Spirit. The priests and the king were all past feeling. These people at one time all knew the truth and were members of the Church. They had fallen into inactivity and into lives of wickedness. Abinadi prophesied and testified to them of their evil ways, and instead of humility and contrite hearts, we see hard hearts and stiff necks. Then we read this: "And now it came to pass that when Abinadi had finished these sayings, that the king commanded that the priests should take him and cause that he should be put to death" (Mosiah 17:1). Abinadi must have felt so alone at this point as he knew it was his time, which makes the next verse so insightful and powerful to me.

"But there was one among them whose name was Alma, he also being a descendant of Nephi. And he was a young man, and he believed the words which Abinadi had spoken, for he knew concerning the iniquity which Abinadi had testified against them; therefore he began to plead with the king" (Mosiah 17:2). Out of the many people in the king's court that day, those who knew what was right, who knew that what the king was doing was wrong, who should have known better, "there was one" who spoke up. I don't know his exact words, but I know it must have been absolutely powerful. I know it may have been spoken with some fear and trepidation, but that only makes it that much more powerful. Where did Alma get the courage? It came from a God who hadn't forgotten His son, Alma.

Here are some thoughts I have about Alma that day (with a little bit of scriptural liberty). He went to work that day like it was any other day. He was expecting to have a normal day, but instead he heard the voice of a prophet and felt something he hadn't felt in a long time. He felt some stirrings, yearnings, impressions, and something inside that said: *I remember these feelings. This man is majestic; he speaks with power, authority, and the Spirit of God. He must be a prophet. I can't keep doing what I am doing or I will keep getting what I am getting. Today is the day, now is the time. I am not going to sit back and watch something that is not right happen anymore.* So, he did something amazing; he stood. He stood and boldly declared truths from his heart. Though scary, it must have felt fantastic to speak with such boldness and power.

I think of all the abused, the picked on, the lonely, and the weary, and I say: they just need one. What if one person stood in a time of crisis? What if one stood in front of a group to inspire them to choose better? What if one young man said "no" to a serious temptation? What if one young woman said "no" in a time of trial? What if one friend told you to stop walking the path you are traveling? What if one young lady opened her mouth to share truth with someone who desperately needed to know the plan? What if one young man boldly defended someone who had become an easy target?

"But there was one" (Mosiah 17:2) will always be a favorite phrase of mine. It has become a goal of mine to be *the one.* I wish that what was written of Alma could be written of me when adversity, temptation, or a trial comes. The question I pose to myself is: when the crowd is intimidating and intense, will I be the one with courage? Will I be able to stand and say, "No, I am not going there"? Will I be able to say, "He is right; don't persecute him for following the Lord"? Will I choose persecution over popularity? Will I choose the Lord, no matter what the price?

President Monson said, years ago, "Life's journey is not traveled on a freeway devoid of obstacles, pitfalls, and snares. Rather, it is a pathway marked by forks and turnings. Decisions are constantly before us. To make them wisely, courage is needed: the courage to say *no,* the courage to say *yes.*"[2] There is great courage that is expected of a servant of the Lord. Remember these words: "Be strong and of a good courage; be not afraid, neither be thou dismayed: for the Lord thy God is with thee whithersoever thou goest" (Joshua 1:9).

I pray that in your mission you will be *the one.* The one who chooses to stand. The one who chooses to defend. The one who chooses to sacrifice social status. The one who chooses to say "but as for me and my house, we will serve the Lord" (Joshua 24:15).

Your friend,
Brother Jeff Erickson

NOTES

1. Carl Bloch, *Peter's Denial*, 41 in. × 33 in.
2. Thomas S. Monson, "Courage Counts," *Ensign* November 1986; emphasis in original.

Finding Strength
beyond Your Own

IRON ROD

Dear Elders and Sisters,

There are times when I am not certain that the scriptures are making it into the hearts of my children. Sometimes our family scripture study feels like an extension of a family napping, as we invite our children to please follow along. Occasionally, however, I witness things that reassure me that some of the words of the prophets are penetrating the hearts and minds of my children. One such occasion occurred when my son Blake was asked to do some jobs around the house. He wasn't motivated, so I encouraged him a second time. His older brother Tanner was observing and assessing the situation. To assist me, Tanner chimed in, spoke in a commanding voice, and said, "Blake, get it done or you'll perish." I don't know that it was the right thing to say, but I walked away humored and feeling better about family scripture study.

As a missionary, by this time, I am certain you have fallen in love with the scriptures. I hope you can convey that love to the people you minister to and that they too may fall in love with the word of God. I want to give you a few more reasons to love the word of God and enjoy the promises you are entitled to as you hold fast to the word. Here is yet another promise from the Book of Mormon: "And I said unto them that it was the word of God; and whoso would hearken unto the word of God, and would hold fast unto it, they would never perish; neither could the temptations and the fiery darts of the adversary overpower them unto blindness, to lead them away to destruction" (1 Nephi 15:24). I have witnessed the power of this promise in my life, and I know this is a true promise from God.

There is incredible power in the word of God. The Lord said to Joseph Smith, "Light and truth forsake that evil one" (D&C 93:37).

The scriptures are filled with light and truth. Faithful study of the word of God will give you power to thwart the wiles of the adversary and fill you with light. Mormon said,

> Yea, we see that whosoever will may lay hold upon the word of God, which is quick and powerful, which shall divide asunder all the cunning and the snares and the wiles of the devil, and lead the man of Christ in a strait and narrow course across that everlasting gulf of misery which is prepared to engulf the wicked.
>
> And land their souls, yea, their immortal souls, at the right hand of God in the kingdom of heaven. (Helaman 3:29–30)

A few winters ago, we were up at Sundance Mountain Resort as a family. It was a fun family trip, and I will never forget one lesson I learned while there. I had a few of my youngest boys with me getting on the ski lift. I remember it vividly because they would get on the lift, and I was immediately nervous for their safety. The front of the lift chair was open, and it was anywhere from a five-foot to a seventy-foot drop off the lift, depending on the location of the chair on the lift route. All of my fears about their safety would dissipate when we would get on the ski lift and pull down the metal safety bar in front of us. Amazingly, one sturdy, well-positioned steel bar alleviated all of my concerns about the safety of my children falling from the chair lift. For me, the metal bar brought peace and protection. I have thought time and time again about that experience. How can something so scary be made so safe?

In studying Lehi's dream, I believe it could have been scary in so many ways—mists of darkness, strange roads, a muddy river, and people laughing and mocking. Even with these tools of the adversary, the iron rod simply made these scary obstacles unimportant factors, if one would just hold to the rod. Holding to the rod and pressing forward overcomes any diversion, deception, or darkness that may come into our lives. Like the iron bar on the ski lift, a loving God placed an iron bar in front of us to protect us spiritually. This iron rod will prevent us from falling into sin if we put it in the right position in our lives.

"Wherefore, I said unto you, feast upon the words of Christ; for behold, the words of Christ will tell you all things what ye should do" (2 Nephi 32:3). I promise you that as you read faithfully, the Lord will

Finding Strength beyond Your Own

tell you of the things you should do as a missionary. He will tell the people you teach what they need to do to follow Him. He will light their paths through His word.

"And it supposeth me that they have come up hither to hear the pleasing word of God, yea, the word which healeth the wounded soul" (Jacob 2:8). The word of God will help to heal the wounds of life that have been heaped upon the people you teach. They will feel the Lord's salve upon their souls as they commit to studying the word of God, especially the Book of Mormon. I remember my years of college at BYU, which were wonderful, but often stressful with frequent tests and deadlines. I remember on many occasions when my stress would peak, I would retreat to the school library to read a chapter or two from the Book of Mormon. These sacred pages caused the Spirit to wash over me and restore peace to my troubled soul during many stressful times.

Here is a final great blessing regarding the word of God and the people you teach: "And this he did that he himself might go forth among his people, or among the people of Nephi, that he might preach the word of God unto them, to stir them up in remembrance of their duty" (Alma 4:19). If you will testify of the word and teach the principles from the scriptures, the Spirit will help your investigators remember who they are and their role in the plan of salvation.

I testify that as you try the virtue of the word of God, it will change your life and the lives of the people you teach. (See Alma 31:5.) I pray that you will feel the Lord's richest blessings and lay claim on His many powerful promises in the scriptures. Joseph Smith Jr. said about the Book of Mormon, "A man would get nearer to God by abiding by its precepts, than by any other book" (Introduction to the Book of Mormon). This promise has been true in my life. Moroni said, "And whoso receiveth this record, and shall not condemn it because of the imperfections which are in it, the same shall know of greater things than these" (Mormon 8:12). Throughout my life, the Lord continues to teach and show me more and more wonderful principles and promises. I pray that you will have your own witness to this principle with the promise that He is currently showing you greater and greater things. May you always remember these wonderful words from the hymnal,

"Hold to the rod, the iron rod; 'Tis strong, and bright, and true. The iron rod is the word of God; 'Twill safely guide us through."[1]

Your friend,
Brother Jeff Erickson

Finding Strength
beyond Your Own

NOTES

1.   The Iron Rod, *Hymns*, 274.

THE GREATNESS OF CAPTAIN MORONI

Dear Elders and Sisters,

When my son Tyler was five years old, I was in the backyard doing some yard work. He was just over the short fence next door playing with the neighbor kids. As I worked, I could hear their conversation. Each child was picking a superhero to be while they played. I heard one choose Batman, and another choose Superman, and then I heard Tyler choose Captain Moroni. I am certain the neighbor boys were puzzled at Tyler's choice as they inquired who Captain Moroni was. I heard young Tyler explain to them that he was a really strong guy. I am grateful that Tyler's boyhood hero is still impacting his life into his twenties.

I know my son Tyler's favorite verse in the Book of Mormon is Mormon's commentary on Moroni: "Yea, verily, . . . If all men had been, and were, and ever would be, like unto Moroni, behold, the very powers of hell would have been shaken forever; yea, the devil would never have power over the hearts of the children of men" (Alma 48:17). Wow! This verse is actually preceded by a few verses that give powerful insights into Moroni's Christlike character:

> And Moroni was a strong and a mighty man; he was a man of perfect understanding; yea, a man that did not delight in bloodshed; a man whose soul did joy in the liberty and the freedom of his country, and his brethren from bondage and slavery;
>
> Yea, a man whose heart did swell with thanksgiving to his God, for the many privileges and blessings which he bestowed upon his people; a man who did labor exceedingly for the welfare and safety of his people.

> Yea, and he was a man who was firm in the faith of Christ, and he had sworn with an oath to defend his people, his rights, and his country, and his religion, even to the loss of his blood. (Alma 48:11–13)

I read those four verses and wonder what else could be said about Moroni. He was righteous, faithful, powerful, selfless, and grateful. He trusted in God for all his blessings. I love that four-verse summary, and I have always read those verses and concluded, "He is awesome." I have learned in my Book of Mormon reading that those verses are insightful and powerful, but they don't tell the whole story. The rest of the chapter shows that Moroni was even greater than those four verses indicate. Let me share some profound insights from earlier in the chapter. I believe these thoughts can apply to your life, your mission, and your future.

In Alma 48:3, Amalackiah (who parallels the adversary) was busy; he was anxiously spreading ill will, hatred, and anger, as well as blinding minds (which means teaching things that are false and misleading). He was busy creating a mess through despair, frustration, and iniquity. He was teaching that wickedness and pride produce happiness, which is never true. The goal of Amalackiah, or the adversary, is shared in the next verse, which is "to bring them into bondage" (Alma 48:4). The scriptures repeatedly teach of bondage and the snare of sin. Bondage will lead to our utter destruction. The goal of Amalackiah, and the adversary, is personal spiritual destruction caused by being bound down by sin and iniquity.

"Moroni, on the other hand, had been preparing the minds of the people to be faithful unto the Lord their God" (Alma 48:7). Moroni's actions in verse seven had a powerful effect on me as I read them. While the world and the forces of the adversary are doing what they are doing, there are good people doing the opposite. Moroni knows what the adversary is trying to do, he knows how destructive the consequences will be, but he is doing everything in his power to get all those who will listen prepared for the coming onslaught of the adversary. He is steady. He is constant. He is not spreading anger or hatred, or blinding minds. He is teaching about preparation, truth, faith, and righteousness.

The next verse tells us, "He had been strengthening the armies of the Nephites" (Alma 48:8). Moroni was strengthening the people by doing what Alma had taught: "And now, as the preaching of the word had a great tendency to lead the people to do that which was just—yea, it had had more powerful effect upon the minds of the people than the sword, or anything else, which had happened unto them—therefore Alma thought it was expedient that they should try the virtue of the word of God" (Alma 31:5). Moroni was teaching them principles of truth and inspiring them to be prepared and strengthened by God.

Moroni continued preparing to "support their liberty . . . their wives, and their children, and their peace . . . the Lord their God . . . [and] the cause of Christians" (Alma 48:10). I love all of that. Moroni knew that liberty is far greater than bondage. Peace is greater than despair. He knew that bondage leads to eternal destruction and death, while freedom leads to prosperity and eternal life. The Lord's way is so much greater than the adversary's way. Moroni knew that their cause was just and right. To these great purposes, Moroni devoted all his energies, even when the enemy was not currently threatening them. Moroni's Christianity was seven days a week, twenty-four hours a day—never only on Sundays.

I have come to love this entire chapter and have found a direct parallel between Moroni's time and your time as a missionary. You are attempting, through the Spirit, to prepare people to battle against the onslaught of evil that is in the world. You are trying to strengthen and free people through true principles and faith in the Lord Jesus Christ. Certainly, there are Amalackiah's out there who are promoting the "cause of the adversary." These people, or groups, fight against Zion, they fight against truth, and they fight against those who are strong and prepared. These adversaries will always be there, but I pray that they will always be defeated as Amalackiah was defeated by faithful servants of God. I know emissaries of Christ who have been preparing the minds of the people and who go about strengthening those they work with and thwarting the work of the adversary.

These verses remind me that as great as Captain Moroni was, he was always selfless. His time and efforts were always courageously and selflessly spent on others. He was a servant first. He understood the Savior's statement perfectly, "But he that is greatest among you shall be your servant" (Matthew 23:11). He truly devoted his entire life to serving Heavenly Father's children. I will always love his attributes, and I

Finding Strength beyond Your Own

know they were given to him because he was absolutely committed to being an instrument in the hands of a loving God. I love Mormon's summary of Moroni, Ammon, Alma, and the sons of Mosiah when he says: "They were all men of God" (Alma 48:18). Truly, Captain Moroni was a man of God.

I know this is one of the great reasons we are called on full-time missions. We are called so that we may develop some of those attributes that Moroni developed as he served. We are called to prepare and strengthen people for the coming of Christ and the defense of righteous principles of truth. We are called, as Moroni was, to preserve freedom. May you forget about yourself and be perfectly selfless in your efforts. May you come closer to Christ, and, as Moroni did, bring others closer to Christ. May you be called a man or woman of God.

Your friend,
Brother Jeff Erickson

Finding Strength
beyond Your Own

CONSECRATE THY PERFORMANCE

Dear Elders and Sisters,

I remember years ago, as a stake missionary, teaching a young sister named Teresa. On this particular night, we felt we should invite her to be baptized. We desperately wanted the Spirit to bear witness to her that she needed to follow Christ and be baptized. We longed for our performance as missionaries to be consecrated by God.

As we taught Teresa, the Lord answered our prayers, and the lesson and room overflowed with the Spirit. We eventually got to the baptismal invitation where we talked of baptism and the sacred gift of the Holy Ghost. We explained how the Holy Ghost would bless her life with guidance and direction on a regular basis. As we discussed the Holy Ghost, Teresa had been feeling His warmth and presence. I remember her excitement when she realized, almost in disbelief, that she could have that gift for herself permanently. She was extremely excited that she could receive this precious gift of the Holy Ghost through baptism.

A few years ago as I read the Book of Mormon, I recorded many of the promises I found. Even though my list was not very comprehensive, there was a multitude of major promises. We believe in a God of principles and promises. We believe in the "if/then" principle. If you are obedient, then God can and will bless you. If you are not obedient, you have no promise. (See D&C 82:10.) As I recorded promises, I discovered that there are numerous principles I had never thought about. On one occasion, I read a promise that made an impression on me during family scripture study. It is one "undiscovered promise" that

I feel I have not utilized enough: "But behold, I say unto you that ye must pray always, and not faint; that ye must not perform any thing unto the Lord save in the first place ye shall pray unto the Father in the name of Christ, that he will consecrate thy performance unto thee, that thy performance may be for the welfare of thy soul" (2 Nephi 32:9). Wow! In the next chapter, Nephi tells us that what he has written is of "great worth" (2 Nephi 33:3).

This phrase from verse nine is certainly of great worth: "Pray always, and not faint." What does that mean? *Faint*, as used by Nephi, means to weaken or fade or to dim. Nephi, then, is saying, pray with strength, with vigor, and with power—not weakly. I have done both before, and the results are so much greater when we pray with power and "faint not." As a missionary, you need to pray with boldness and directness. If you are obedient, you can ask much of the Lord. For instance, "Heavenly Father, I need this person to receive a witness. I need them to feel the Spirit, and I need a miracle." These are all appropriate requests when one is worthy. Remember to pray with power for the people you teach, for your companions, for the work, for more opportunities, and for the wards and branches you are in.

This second phrase from 2 Nephi 32:9 is also critical: "Ye must not perform any thing unto the Lord save in the first place ye shall pray unto the Father in the name of Christ." Don't do anything as a missionary without praying first. It is the Lord's word. Ask for help, guidance, strength, discipline, patience, and love. Ask for any gift you desire that is right, and He will grant it to you. Remember, it is the work of God, and you are an instrument, so you must recognize your dependence on Him and on His Spirit. Pray about anything and everything. Just pray!

The last two phrases are my points of emphasis in verse nine: "He will consecrate thy performance" and "Thy performance may be for the welfare of thy soul." Starting with the first phrase: "He will consecrate thy performance." What does that mean? Will He make my teaching more Spirit-filled? Will He fill my mouth with the words that I should say? Will He help me pronounce more powerful priesthood blessings? Will He help my companion and me know who to visit and prompt us to see the right person at the right time? Will He help us know what area to tract in and what door to knock on? Will He help me to overcome the fear I have of testifying to others? Will He help me get out of bed on time? Will He help me study the things that I will need that very day? Will He help me listen to the Spirit and heed its promptings? Will He help me literally be the voice of an angel? Will He help me be bold, but not overbearing? Will He help me be a humble servant? Will He help me ask the appropriate inspired question when teaching? Will He tell me what message would benefit my investigator the most? The answer to all the above is: Yes, Yes, Yes!

Consecrate is another powerful word. What does it mean? It means He will bless, sanctify, make sacred, or make holy your performance. I testify that God will consecrate your performance as you pray always. You will feel, see, and know there is a difference when you pray more earnestly. The promise is that He will "consecrate thy performance" for the welfare of your soul (and for the souls of others). As you pray for a consecrated performance, may you turn your life over to God and watch as he changes your heart, sanctifies you, and blesses you more than you ever dreamed.

President Kimball approached life and serving in the kingdom with diligence and love. The Lord consecrated his performance as he made President Kimball powerful. There is a wonderful story told by President Kimball's secretary that is worth repeating here.

> We went to a conference in the eastern United States where President Kimball met a man who had the same last name. The missionaries had been teaching him the gospel, and when he learned that his cousin Spencer was coming to town, he "adopted" the President and was with us nearly every minute that we were in the city. He became very fond of President Kimball and was impressed with his work and his spirit. He rode to the airport with us, and on the way he turned to me and offered the highest compliment that he could imagine, which came from his own church background. He said, "Your church ought to make my cousin Spencer a saint."
>
> President Kimball was riding in the front seat, but he overheard what had been said. He turned around quickly and said, "Nobody can make me a saint. I have to do that for myself."[1]

One day, a good woman named Kim, who was not a member of the Church, was having some serious marital struggles. She had many trials at the time, and a good friend of hers who was in our ward, wanted her to get a priesthood blessing. We knew Kim because she had been a friend of the family for a few years. The arrangements were made for me to give Kim a priesthood blessing. I remember feeling that Kim was prepared for the gospel, and I remember pleading desperately that she would feel something from the blessing. The Lord consecrated my prayer and the priesthood blessing that day when Kim had a powerful experience during the blessing. She later stated that during the blessing she felt the Spirit of God and the hand of God touch her life. What a blessing it was for me to be a voice for Heavenly Father and to be a small instrument in Kim's life.

This priesthood blessing moved Kim as it strengthened her in a significant time of need. A few weeks following the priesthood blessing, Kim began taking the missionary lessons. Through the lesson process, Kim received another witness of the truthfulness of the gospel of Jesus Christ. It was just a few weeks after the "priesthood experience" that Kim was baptized into the Church. I remember feeling so blessed as I watched Heavenly Father work His miracle in the life of this sweet, prepared sister.

Years ago when Agnes Bojaxhiu (Mother Teresa) made the decision to become a nun, her brother, Lazar, presented some opposition. Lazar was serving in the Albanian army when he wrote to her and challenged her decision. She wrote this reply to him, "You think you are important because you are an officer serving a king with two million subjects. But I am serving the King of the whole world."[2] Always remember that you are serving the king of the universe, and that He will consecrate your performance if you ask Him to. I pray for your success. I pray your performance will be consecrated.

Your friend,
Brother Jeff Erickson

Powerful Prayer

NOTES

1. D. Arthur Haycock, "He Went about Doing Good," *Ensign*, December 1985.
2. Kathryn Spink, *Mother Theresa: An Authorized Biography* (New York: HarperCollins, 2011), 11.

MISSIONARY PRAYER

Dear Elders and Sisters,

I remember a day when I offered one of the most heartfelt prayers I had ever offered in my life. It was Saturday, and my sons were doing their chores outside. I was inside doing some work when I started to look around the house for my little two-year-old daughter. I could not find her anywhere, and then I walked in the kitchen and saw that the back door was open. I went into the yard and found that my son had propped the pool gate open, which violated every family rule we had, and he was nowhere to be found. I saw the gate, and my heart sunk. I began to beg in a prayer that she was not in the pool. I sprinted for the pool as my prayers and pleadings became more fervent. I remember saying, "Please, no, Heavenly Father." I continued to plead with God as I scanned the pool area, and relief washed over me when I discovered that she was not in the pool. A few minutes later, and after a little more searching, I found her in a remote part of the house.

I want to study the heartfelt plea Alma offered as he was going on yet another mission. For this mission, he took the best missionaries he knew and possibly the best missionaries the Church ever knew. He knew the work was going to be in a difficult "area," and he knew there would be great adversity. He also knew the work would be hard, the people not very receptive, and he knew there would be disappointment and discouragement. In addition, he was aware that he couldn't save every soul and that not everyone would listen. He was very aware and very realistic as he pleaded for God's help. For those reasons, I love his pleadings with the Lord; they are powerful and an example of what all full-time missionaries (and members) should pray for and about.

By way of a reminder, remember that Alma and his zone of missionaries have just watched the Zoramites pray upon the Rameumptom

(Alma 31:12–22). These people were far from righteous, but Alma believed there were some humble and truth-seeking individuals among them. Here are a few of the verses that I believe our prayers, specifically those of a missionary preparing to go full-time and preach with all his might in a difficult setting, should echo.

> O Lord God, how long wilt thou suffer that such wickedness and infidelity shall be among this people? O Lord, wilt thou give me strength, that I may bear with mine infirmities. For I am infirm, and such wickedness among this people doth pain my soul.
>
> O Lord, my heart is exceedingly sorrowful; wilt thou comfort my soul in Christ. O Lord, wilt thou grant unto me that I may have strength, that I may suffer with patience these afflictions which shall come upon me, because of the iniquity of this people.
>
> O Lord, wilt thou comfort my soul, and give unto me success, and also my fellow laborers who are with me—yea, Ammon, and Aaron, and Omner, and also Amulek and Zeezrom and also my two sons—yea, even all these wilt thou comfort, O Lord. Yea, wilt thou comfort their souls in Christ.
>
> Wilt thou grant unto them that they may have strength, that they may bear their afflictions which shall come upon them because of the iniquities of this people.
>
> O Lord, wilt thou grant unto us that we may have success in bringing them again unto thee in Christ.
>
> Behold, O Lord, their souls are precious, and many of them are our brethren; therefore, give unto us, O Lord, power and wisdom that we may bring these, our brethren, again unto thee. (Alma 31:30–35)

I love the desire that comes through in his words as he pleads with the Lord to bring these people to Christ. When I read the desires of Alma's heart as he begins his service, it makes me want to plead for souls more fervently. I don't know if there is a greater missionary prayer in all of scripture. When I read his words, I see the depth of his love, his understanding, and his love of his companions. I know that his goals align with the goals of God. I hope that every missionary can feel what Alma felt, desire what he desired, and appeal to God as sincerely as Alma did.

The most beautiful part of Alma's whole prayer is that these blessings, his pleadings, were realized. Alma and his zone of missionaries were blessed with success, not immediately, but they found the elect

Powerful Prayer

who were willing to listen. They taught the honest in heart when they found them, and had great success. May Alma's prayer be an inspiration to you as you do God's will. May you, as Alma did, plead for strength, power, and wisdom, and may a loving and merciful Heavenly Father bless you with success as He did with Alma.

Recently, in the newspaper, there was an account of a man that posed as a religious pastor. He was a businessman who made seven million dollars over the course of four years. He had over 1.2 million likes on his Facebook page; he had hundreds of thousands of people pay for his services, anywhere from nine dollars to thirty-five dollars. What were the services he was offering? He was offering "pay for prayer" requests: to have ministers, religious leaders, and Christians pray for individuals and people who needed divine help with a variety of problems, concerns, and conditions. These people requesting and paying for these "prayers" wanted small miracles granted from God through someone who would pray for their needs.

After four years of considerable financial gain, he was arrested for falsifying claims, testimonials, and his credentials and the credentials of other supposed religious leaders. What does this experience about people desperately wanting prayers in their behalf and in behalf of their loved ones teach us? One principle is that people desperately want God's influence in their lives, and they want Him to intervene in their behalf.[1]

What a blessing we have as Latter-day Saints, and as missionaries, to know how to request God's intervention in our lives and feel His influence in answer to personal prayers filled with faith. I am so grateful for the price of prayer, and that it is not measured in dollars, but in desires. I pray that we as missionaries may have Alma-like desires as we plead for success in our labors.

Your friend,
Brother Jeff Erickson

NOTES

1. Enjoli Francis, Neal Karlinsky, and Michael Mendelsohn, "Owner of 'Pay to Pray' Website Ordered to Return $7.8M to Consumers," *ABC News*, March 17, 2016.

Powerful Prayer

PRAY ALWAYS

Dear Elders and Sisters,

One year, my sons and I went to our ward's annual father-and-sons outing in the Pinal Mountains of Arizona. We were driving to the peak of the mountain, which meant we were on a road with sheer cliffs on one side. My boys could see over the edge in some instances and were afraid on the drive to the peak. They urged me constantly to slow down, but I was already traveling at a very safe speed. The next morning, on the way back down the mountain, we had a prayer before we left. My young son Blake offered it, and I will never forget his honest and sincere words. He prayed, "Heavenly Father, bless us that we won't go over the edge." His words hit home for me, and we stayed as far from the edge on the way down as we could, and we never went over.

In the Church, there are many inspiring phrases that we hear either in songs, from our leaders, or in Primary or Sunday school. There are phrases like "do it now," "return with honor," "stand a little taller," "choose the right," "teach me to walk in the light," "be true," "stand for truth and righteousness," and many other inspiring thoughts. I know missionaries have many slogans, mottoes, catch phrases, or quotes that they use to motivate and inspire themselves and their companions in laboring in the kingdom. I submit yet one more to you that I hope changes and blesses your life immensely. One of the greatest phrases in all scripture is "pray always." I believe these two words are used together twelve times in the Doctrine and Covenants.

Why is "pray always" such a powerful phrase? Every time it is used in the scriptures, it is followed by absolutely wonderful promises from our loving Heavenly Father who always wants to bless us and see us prosper. This phrase, and its promises, should be a means for a missionary to pray down the powers of heaven. Here are some of the promises we see in the scriptures if we pray always:

- "*Pray always*, that you may come off conqueror; yea, that you may conquer Satan, and that you may escape the hands of the servants of Satan that do uphold his work" (D&C 10:5). Wow! Pray to be delivered from the destroyer and even to conquer him. Through prayer, you will escape his clutches and his snares.

- "*Pray always*, and I will pour out my Spirit upon you, and great shall be your blessing—yea, even more than if you should obtain treasures of earth and corruptibleness to the extent thereof" (D&C 19:38). Double wow! The imagery of being completely drenched with the Spirit is both powerful and wonderful. As a missionary, is there anything you need more than the Spirit? Missionaries must pray always to be filled with the Spirit; there is no greater treasure for a full-time missionary.

- "Therefore let the church take heed and *pray always*, lest they fall into temptation" (D&C 20:33). Praying always will help you from falling into temptation. Missionaries, like everyone else, are tempted, and prayer will protect you from those temptations.

- "And they shall give heed to that which is written, and pretend to no other revelation; and they shall *pray always* that I may unfold the same to their understanding" (D&C 32:4). If you pray always, understanding will be given unto you. The Lord teaches us when we pray and ask. There are so many principles and doctrines that the Lord can teach us through prayer and the Spirit if we will allow Him.

- "*Pray always* that they faint not; and inasmuch as they do this, I will be with them even unto the end." (D&C 75:11). As missionaries, if you pray always, you will not *faint* (weaken, dim, or fade). You will press forward

Powerful Prayer

with steadfastness in Christ because you are praying always. I also love the promise that if you pray always, Christ will be with you until the end; this means until the end of your mission, your life, and your eternal life. Praying daily is critical for strength and salvation.

- "Search diligently, *pray always*, and be believing, and all things shall work together for your good, if ye walk uprightly and remember the covenant wherewith ye have covenanted one with another" (D&C 90:24). This promise is combined with other contingencies, but the promise alone is tremendous: all things shall work together for your good. That is a promise for the obedient. Prayer is a critical aspect of obedience. If you will seek Heavenly Father frequently in prayer, all things shall work for your good.

- "What I say unto one I say unto all; *pray always* lest that wicked one have power in you, and remove you out of your place" (D&C 93:49). If you don't want the adversary to destroy your life with the chains of habit or darkness, pray always. In the Book of Mormon, we are also taught that Satan will have no power over the hearts of the righteous; the righteous "pray always."

I have briefly skimmed the surface with a few powerful promises surrounding one simple phrase. It's evident to me that there is something wonderful about prayer. I don't know if it's because it is a commandment of God or if it's because we acknowledge God when we pray. I don't know if it's because prayer causes us to remember Him or if it's because we can draw upon the powers of heaven when we pray. I don't know if it's because revelation comes after prayer. I am not certain of the "whys," but I know praying always works. For missionaries, if you will pray always, the richness of heaven will be poured down upon you and you truly will be filled with the blessings of God.

Your friend,
Brother Jeff Erickson

Powerful Prayer

ASTONISHED BEYOND MEASURE

Dear Elders and Sisters,

My wife and I were sitting in the living room with our son Tanner, who was almost four at the time. Tanner already had two brothers, and we were talking to him about our new baby that would be coming in a few months. Tanner was now old enough to be impressed by Mom's sacrifices during her pregnancy and her ability to bring babies home from the hospital. Needless to say, little Tanner was astonished at what Mom had gone through and done for him to have brothers. He was excited to have a new brother, and was grateful for his mom in bringing this new brother into the world. He looked at me—almost with disgust—and said "Dad, when are you going to have a baby?"

There is a beautiful verse in the Book of Mormon that reminds me of the blessings of serving a full-time mission: "And so great was the prosperity of the church, and so many the blessings which were poured out upon the people, that even the high priests and the teachers were themselves astonished beyond measure" (Helaman 3:25). Have you ever felt "astonished beyond measure" for the many blessings you have received from the hand of the Lord?

I remember moments on my mission when I was able to feel the Spirit in such abundance that I was "astonished beyond measure." I remember singing "Onward Christian Soldiers" as the closing song of the baptism of my first convert, Jim. I remember not being able to sing the words because I was too overcome with emotion. I felt an extra portion of the Spirit and was "astonished beyond measure" at the love God had for me and for this man who had completely changed his life after feeling the love of God. He had been converted in an astonishing manner. This good man was now devoted to Christ, and, for this, his life was about to be blessed "beyond measure."

The only other time in the scriptures that this phrase, or one similar to it, is used in this positive context is in the New Testament. Mark is speaking of Christ with the multitude who "were beyond measure astonished, saying, He hath done all things well: he maketh both the deaf to hear, and the dumb to speak" (Mark 7:37). I love this commentary because it echoes how I feel in my life about the Savior. I am "astonished beyond measure" at the love He has for us, at the goodness I feel from His hand, at the constant blessings He pours down upon us, and for the Atonement, which He has wrought in our behalf.

In an article by Daniel Petersen, he tells of an additional witness to the golden plates, besides the eleven whose testimony is written in the front of the Book of Mormon. The name of witness number twelve is Mary Musselman Whitmer. I tell her story because I believe she was "astonished beyond measure."

John C. Whitmer, her grandson, reported that he himself had heard his grandmother tell of this event several times. He summarized her experience as follows:

> She met a stranger carrying something on his back that looked like a knapsack. At first she was a little afraid of him, but when he spoke to her in a kind, friendly tone and began to explain to her the nature of the work which was going on in her house (that is, the translation of the Book of Mormon), *she was filled with unexpressible* [sic] *joy and satisfaction.* He then untied his knapsack and showed her a bundle of plates, which in size and appearance corresponded with the description subsequently given by the witnesses to the Book of Mormon. This strange person turned the leaves of the book of plates over, leaf after leaf, and also showed her the engravings upon them; after which he told her to be patient and faithful in bearing her burden a little longer, promising that if she would do so, she should be blessed; and her reward would be sure, if she proved faithful to the end. The personage then suddenly vanished with the plates, and where he went, she could not tell."[1]

I can relate to Sister Mary Whitmer as I have had experiences where I was filled with "unexpressible *[sic]* joy" and was "astonished beyond measure." When you have experiences and sacred moments as a missionary, I hope you will remember to express gratitude for them. I hope you will always remember where they came from.

I also hope that as you teach, minister, and love the people of your area, you will help them to be exceedingly astonished at the goodness of God and the wonderful principles that you exemplify in the gospel of Jesus Christ. I am impressed that even a man like Lamoni's father, who appeared to have a hardened heart, could be profoundly affected by the love that comes through the gospel of Jesus Christ: "And when he saw that Ammon had no desire to destroy him, and when he also saw the great love he had for his son Lamoni, he was astonished exceedingly" (Alma 20:26).

When we, as missionaries, focus on the goodness of God and the many rich blessings of our missions, we will help others to be "astonished beyond measure." I remember being an instructor in the missionary training center and teaching a young missionary named Elder Lacey. He was struggling with his testimony, and he was practicing teaching the Joseph Smith story in the classroom. Suddenly, as he was teaching and testifying of Joseph Smith, he felt the Spirit encompass him and, for the first time in his young life, he knew that Joseph Smith was a prophet of God. He quickly pulled me into the hallway, his eyes wet with tears as he hugged me and excitedly said, "I know Joseph Smith is a prophet." The Spirit had astonished him beyond measure.

A few years ago, I was up late holding one of my little sons, who had fallen asleep in my arms while I rocked him in the rocking chair. I was pondering all the blessings God had given my wife and me. I remember being completely overcome by the Spirit and being filled with the love of God for my little family. It was a simple, yet very treasured, experience that I will never forget. I was truly "astonished beyond measure" for the blessing of my precious family.

May you on your mission do what Nephi did and come to a knowledge of the "goodness . . . of God" (1 Nephi 1:1) as He blesses and astonishes you "beyond measure" (Helaman 3:25).

Your friend,
Brother Jeff Erickson

NOTES

1.   Daniel Peterson, "Defending the Faith: Mary Whitmer, 12th witness to the Book of Mormon," *Deseret News*, July 18, 2013, www.deseretnews.com /article/865583267/; emphasis added.

Promised Blessings

EYE OF FAITH

Dear Elders and Sisters,

One Sunday morning, my son Blake got up for church and didn't like some of the clothes he was wearing. He absolutely refused to wear the big brown shoes that were supposed to be his church shoes. He said they were goofy and that he hated them. I looked at the shoes and noticed that they looked a little like a pair of shoes I had worn many years ago. I told Blake that his shoes were like some "waffle stompers" that I used to wear when I was a kid. I told him my "waffle stompers" were some of the best shoes I ever had. I looked at his shoes and declared them as being "awesome." I said to Blake, "I love those! Where did you get those? Why don't you always wear those?" I continued on by telling him other things he could do with them, including smashing bugs. I concluded by saying, "They really do look nice." After a few minutes of convincing, Blake soon believed the shoes were great. He then said, "Hey, they do look nice." The pinnacle of the conversion was when Blake sincerely said, "Dad, can I wear these everyday?" Later that day, Blake showed me how fast he could run in them and said he loved his brown shoes. He asked me one more time what they were called. This experience with Blake was a reminder of the importance of adjusting our perspective and seeing things in a more beneficial light.

Alma said, "Do ye exercise faith in the redemption of him who created you? Do you look forward with an eye of faith?" (Alma 5:15). The phrase "eye of faith" has become a favorite of mine. Do we look at situations on our missions through the window of faith in Jesus Christ? Seeing an experience with an eye of faith gives purpose, meaning, and value to everything that happens to us in our lives. When we view our lives and our mission with an eye of faith, we see things with more clarity and depth than ever before. Like Blake, when we see things in a better light, our experiences are much better. We begin to see things from a more godlike perspective. We start to see the rainbows in the storms and the lessons in adversity. We feel peace when despair is all around us. Looking forward with an eye of faith fills us with hope and charity. With an eye of faith, we begin to see as God sees. With an eye of faith, our entire souls can be filled with light. The Savior said, "The light of the body is the eye: if therefore thine eye be single, thy whole body shall be full of light" (Matthew 6:22).

Elder David B. Haight said the following when he was ninety-four years old: "He [President Hinckley] also knows that my eyesight isn't very good, but as my eyesight dims somewhat, I think my vision improves—my vision of the long road, my vision of what lies ahead."[1] As missionaries, you are much younger than Elder Haight was in that general conference, but what if you could honestly say that your vision is improving? I hope everyday as you testify of the principles of the gospel of Jesus Christ that your spiritual acuity is becoming sharper. One young convert sister who had heard the missionaries said, "As they taught with the Spirit, 'it seemed like they had taken the bandages off my eyes and that the Lord was clearing my understanding.'"[2] There is a wonderful amplification and clarity of our vision when we see life through the gospel of Jesus Christ.

One night, many years ago, it was bedtime for my little son McKay. He was exhausted and his eyes were shutting against his will, but he still refused to go to bed. I said, "McKay, you better go to sleep." He responded, "I am not tired—my eyes are just tired." As missionaries, like McKay, you will be physically tired, but never let your eyes get spiritually tired. You need to spiritually see, with clarity, the things that God is trying to show you.

Many years ago, Elder Alma Sonne, who was an assistant to Council of the Twelve, told a story of a man who had witnessed an accident. The man was being grilled by a sarcastic lawyer about what he "saw."

The lawyer said, "Did you see the accident?" The witness replied, "Yes, sir."
"How far away were you?"
The witness said, "Oh, about thirty feet."

"Well, how far can you see anyway?"

He said, "I do not know, but in the morning when I wake up I can see the sun, and they tell me it is about ninety million miles away."[3]

What if every missionary realized that they could see the "Son" every morning when they woke up? A great question we can ask ourselves is: how much faith am I seeing things with each day?

Moroni recounts for us observations of people he knew with great faith. He said of them, "And there were many whose faith was so exceedingly strong even before Christ came, who could not be kept from within the veil, but truly saw with their eyes the things which they had beheld with an eye of faith, and they were glad" (Ether 12:19). This gladness and these rich experiences can only come through strong faith in Jesus Christ. When we have an eye of faith, we are focused on the light rather than the darkness. When we have an eye of faith, we can see the bigger picture. When we have an eye of faith, we become more merciful. When we see with an eye of faith, we are filled with the love of God.

Elder Hanks shared this story in conference:

> This family has a tradition of educational accomplishment and the father was shaken a bit when his wife brought him their high school son's report card with his first *C* on it. Dad brooded over the matter and when the son came home invited him into the study, sternly confronted him with the card, and said, "Son, what is this I see on your report card?"
>
> "Well, Dad," replied the boy, "I *hope* you see the five *A*s."[4]

One of the greatest requests ever recorded in scripture occurred when the Savior taught His disciples about forgiveness. I love their response: "And the apostles said unto the Lord, Increase our faith" (Luke 17:5). For me their plea is, "Lord, help me to see better. Please help me see with an eye of faith." I hope that as a missionary you go to the Lord and ask Him to increase your faith. When that prayer is answered, you will see an increase in your vision, and you will see with more focus the wonderful blessings of the gospel of Jesus Christ. You will then see things, which can only be beheld with an eye of faith, and you will be glad. Remember the prayer of my young son Talmage one night after a family home evening lesson on having an "eye of faith."

He prayed very sincerely, "Heavenly Father, bless us that we don't go blind."

Your friend,
Brother Jeff Erickson

NOTES

1. David B. Haight, "Be a Strong Link," *Ensign*, November 2000.
2. Vicki F. Matsumori "A Lesson from the Book of Mormon," *Ensign*, May 2007.
3. Alma Sonne, *Conference Report*, April 1957, 25.
4. Marion D. Hanks, "Seeing the Five A's," *Ensign*, November 1977; emphasis in original.

"I WILL GIVE UNTO YOU SUCCESS"

Dear Elders and Sisters,

I was reviewing a few missionary-related scriptures as I was writing my son Tyler, and I fell in love with this verse in Alma. In Alma 26, Ammon is rejoicing with his brothers as he is finally coming home from his mission after fourteen years (and you thought eighteen months or two years was long). I love the insights of Ammon since we often think the sons of Mosiah's missions were all about success—baptizing thousands of people and sitting there teaching only golden contacts. It was very different than that. This verse is a vivid reminder of how human these missionaries were, and how much like your mission their mission was. "Now when our hearts were depressed, and we were about to turn back, behold, the Lord comforted us, and said: Go amongst thy brethren, the Lamanites, and bear with patience thine afflictions, and I will give unto you success" (Alma 26:27). These missionaries were instruments in seeing numerous people come into the Church, and sometimes, we think they had it easy with no rejections or disappointments, but that was not the case. The lesson from this verse is that a mission is full of adversity, but when adversity is addressed appropriately, the results equal success. We see through this verse that the sons of Mosiah's missions were full of difficulty and trials, but they were also rewarded with successes.

The word *depressed* stirs in my mind when I read the revealing phrase "about to turn back." It sounds like these were normal missionaries who wanted to go home on occasion—even wanted to give up and questioned if their mission was worth the sacrifice of being away from their friends and family. It sounds like they had bad days just like the rest of us do. I love knowing that they were human, and they had to endure and be mentally strong. They truly struggled like missionaries today do. I feel their humanity when it says they were "about to turn back." I think we have all had some of those days on our missions. There are days when we ask, "why?" That is normal—even Ammon did it.

If the first half of the verse is revealing, the second half is equally as insightful. The last half is the principle with the promise. I have learned that there is nothing better than principles with promises. I have learned that Heavenly Father never breaks promises and that He offers them freely. "Behold, the Lord comforted us, and said . . . bear with patience thine afflictions, and I will give unto you success" (Alma 26:27). I am encouraged by the Lord's promise of comfort. Every missionary will be afflicted to some level; missions are not easy, but they are wonderful. They can be a mental and physical battle. They can be full of heartache and disappointment, but the joys they offer are so much deeper and fulfilling than the sorrows. When you are afflicted, the Lord will comfort you.

Finally, the second promise, "I will give unto you success." That is a guarantee to every missionary from our loving Father. What is the success the Lord promises? It can come in reactivation, in baptisms, or in gaining the love and trust of the members. It can come in seeing the hearts of people change, whether converted or not. It can come in inspiring your companion or other missionaries in your district, zone, or mission. That success can come personally in your own testimony and spiritual growth. The success can come in the peace and joy you feel as you serve faithfully.

As a young missionary, my companion and I taught a college student by the name of Aaron. He was bright, inquisitive, and seemed to want to know the truth. We had many lessons with him. He wanted to believe, but told us he had received no answer. We went to his home one day and retaught him the story of Joseph Smith from Joseph Smith—History. The lesson was powerful, and the Spirit was overwhelming. We invited Aaron to pray and ask God to let him know whether or not Joseph was a prophet and if the Church of Jesus Christ of Latter-day

Saints was true. He offered a very simple, heartfelt prayer. After a few seconds of praying, he was completely overcome by the Spirit, and he couldn't continue. The Spirit of God completely melted his spirit. He sobbed as he felt God's presence answering his prayer. After a minute or two, he regained his composure and closed his sincere prayer by saying, "Thank you for letting me know this is the true church." We then committed Aaron to a baptismal date.

This experience with Aaron was one of the most powerful experiences of my mission. Aaron never did get baptized while I was on my mission. Was this still a success? Yes, because the experience forever changed my companion and me. The lessons learned from that sacred hour with Aaron that day in a small apartment will forever be embedded in my heart. Truly, this was one of the most successful hours of my entire life.

The promise Ammon speaks of in Alma 26 is real, and it will bless you in the work and in your mission. Go amongst the people you serve, be faithful, and bear what you need to bear. The Lord will comfort you, and then bless you with success. Of course, like any principle with a promise, there is the matter of doing your part. I pray you will do your part so you will see and feel the Lord's hand in your labors and in His work. I pray that you will be an effective instrument in the Lord's hands. There is nothing greater than working for Him, in His way, and with His Spirit. Let Him guide and direct you in your labors. Pray for inspiration and direction, and let His light direct your paths.

Your friend,
Brother Jeff Erickson

ABOUT THE AUTHOR

Jeffrey "Jeff" Erickson has been a youth speaker at EFY and a bishop. He has a passion for writing and speaking about the gospel of Jesus Christ, especially to youth. He has published a youth-related story in the *New Era* called "Catch." Jeff has written over 250 weekly letters of encouragement to missionaries all over the world. As he began writing a book for teenagers, he realized that he had already written a complete volume to young missionaries via his weekly letters. As a young man, Jeff served a full-time mission in the Canada Halifax Mission. Jeff and his wife, Christine, have six sons and one daughter.

Scan to visit

www.missionaryletter.com